COMPUTER CRASHES

COMPUTER CRASHES

WHEN AIRPLANE SYSTEMS FAIL

TOM DIEUSAERT

Dieusaert, Tom
Computer crashes: when airplane systems fail / Tom Dieusaert ; adapted by
Tom Buckley. – 1st illustrated edition. – Buenos Aires: Prensa Nueva, 2017.
155 p.; 6 x 9 inches (22 x 14.5 cm).

ISBN 978-987-24843-4-7
CDD 387.7

Cover illustration: Dimitri Axiotis
Cover design: Daniel Graffe
Lay out: Pilar de Uribelarrea and Annelies Verheyden
Contact the author: tomdieusaert@gmail.com
ISBN 978-987-24843-4-7

TABLE OF CONTENT

INTRODUCTION

In June 2009 I was preparing for a holiday in Europe with my daughter. We were getting ready to travel from our home in Buenos Aires when I heard of the Air France crash over the Atlantic Ocean. As we were going to fly the same route with the same airline, the headlines occupied my attention. I followed the news and speculation with more than usual concern.

At first, there were rumors that the plane that disappeared on June 1 off the coast of northern Brazil had been the victim of a bomb attack. The violent drug gangs of Rio de Janeiro were suspected in this scenario, but this hypothesis was discarded quickly, once the remains of the plane found a few days later showed the aircraft had hit the ocean in one piece. What happened to Air France Flight 447? What caused the crash?

It was a real mystery because the state-of-the-art Airbus 330-200 had suffered no apparent malfunction and it was unthinkable that this sophisticated aircraft could simply fall out of the sky. The first credible reports – coming from Air France and Airbus – cited malfunctioning pitot tubes (see Glossary page 188), as the cause of the accident. This puzzled me.

For instance, if a car had a malfunctioning speedometer, would it crash into a tree? I didn't see the relationship. At most, the

11

pilots might have been confused about their speed, but they were evidently flying comfortably at cruise speed and altitude. Why would a minor failure result in such a dramatic outcome?

A member of my rowing club in Buenos Aires, Eduardo "Humpty" Neumann, had enjoyed a long career as senior purser on the national airline Aerolíneas Argentinas. He was also a licensed commercial pilot who flew small airplanes and helicopters, often spending hours at home training in his simulator and watching flight videos on YouTube. He had even helped a younger club member become a pilot. "Humpty" was as close to an old school pilot as one could get to know, often sporting a Top Gun leather jacket with sewn-on badges included.

One night as he completed his daily workout in the gym, I asked him about the incident. "I don't know the details of the Air France case well," he said, "but the explanation of the pitot tubes doesn't convince me."

"What do you mean?" I asked. "That's what the official investigators are saying. How could the malfunctioning speedometers influence the flight path and cause the plane to crash?"

"For me," Neumann continued, "now this is complete speculation because the real causes can't be known until the black box is recovered, but this crash had something to do *with the computers.*"

I was stunned. "The computers?" I said.

"Yes. Modern planes – especially Airbuses – are loaded with computers and sometimes those systems break down or stop working, just like computers do in every day life," he said matter-of-factly. "There are backups, but still, I think this tragedy has something to do with them… In the end, we might never know the truth, because typically the pilot gets the blame. He's dead and cannot defend himself.

"The problem with these computers today is they control the airplane and they limit pilot action. So it has become very hard for the pilot to control the plane manually."

This system is called fly-by-wire (see Glossary page 184), Neumann told me, and it originated with military aircraft. I was learning a lot of new concepts here. I had never heard of fly-by-wire before, though at the time I knew little about aviation. That all changed after June 1, 2009.

Neumann's observations opened up a whole new world. As far as I knew, the only onboard computer was the Auto Pilot that is supposed to relieve the pilots of routine tasks between take-off and landing, the two most critical parts of a flight. I figured it was similar to how an automobile driver would program the vehicle to drive at a certain speed over a long stretch of highway. Now, I understand that this construct is outdated. Computers govern commercial aircraft in such a manner that a pilot's task has become very limited.

"Actually a pilot nowadays flies within a so-called 'flight envelope'," Neumann explained. "He has very little impact on what the plane is doing and this evolution has enhanced safety, because a pilot cannot do crazy climbs, dives and turns as you might see at an air show. On the other hand, when something does go wrong, often the pilots lose control."

If we return to the comparison of automobiles, comfort is a major sales pitch for the growing automation in vehicles. GPS navigation systems have replaced the traditional folded-up map in the glove compartment. In the near future, a self-driving car will drive us from point A to point B without requiring any input from the "driver," who can relax and text on his cell phone. The industry insists these self-driving cars will make traffic safer because maximum speed can be perfectly controlled, navigation will be programmed and sensors will help prevent collisions. Take the man out of the machine and everything works better seems to be the philosophy. This evolution will soon take place in aviation too. Self-flying planes appear imminent.

In the United Arab Emirates, autonomous drones – or self-flying taxis – will fly passengers around the city of Dubai by early 2018. In the UK, British defense company BAE systems is currently testing self-flying planes in a bid to pave the way for unmanned commercial flights by 2020.

Big aircraft constructors like Boeing and Airbus are also developing self-flying planes but have not yet launched unmanned jets. There is a critical psychological factor of leaving passengers in the hands of a computer or an operator monitoring the plane from the ground. Few people would be willing to get on a plane without the trusted figure of the pilot sitting up front.

To a large extent, computers are already in charge of planes. Sometimes they act contrary to the will of the pilots; sometimes these computers behave erratically or even malfunction. "What the hell is it doing?" is a familiar phrase heard in many cockpit conversations. This is quite a distressing fact, not well-known to the public, especially because aviation journalists tend to echo the information fed to them by the big aircraft constructors and national safety board reports.

My conversation with Neumann sparked my own journalistic investigation of a series of air tragedies caused by computer failures. I realized there were many cases of fatal accidents or near-fatal incidents involving onboard computers and, in most cases, the airlines and airplane constructors minimized their responsibility, instead placing the blame on the pilots.

This attitude of denial poses an important risk to passenger safety. We are after all talking about a multi-billion-dollar industry. Massive recalls of an aircraft model are considered unfeasible and potentially a financial disaster. So manufacturers are reluctant to admit design faults on their machines and this could potentially lead to accidents in the future.

There is also an inherent conflict of interest. Modern aircraft design has become so sophisticated that the people most capable of discovering the cause of a crash are the aircraft manufacturers themselves. It would be deemed an outrageous ethical violation if automobile manufacturers themselves were in charge of investigating fraudulent emissions schemes, poorly designed batteries or defective airbags in new models. But this is exactly what is happening in the aviation industry. The recovery of the Flight 447 wreck was conducted by Air France and Airbus, the very same companies involved in the crash.

The case of Air France Flight 447 inspired my research into modern air tragedies, crashes not caused by pilot error or a mechanical malfunction, but those caused by badly designed computer systems that act directly on the controls of the aircraft. I spoke with aircraft crash investigators, seasoned pilots and specialized lawyers. I learned quite a lot about aeronautics, airplane design and the terminology of the industry. To help readers understand some of the more complex issues addressed herein, there is a glossary at the end of the book.

My investigation took me from Brazil to France where I talked with family members of Flight 447 victims, then pointed me back to 1989 when the first fly-by-wire plane crashed in Habsheim, France. It also led me to take a closer look at accidents that happened in the Far East in 2014 including AirAsia Flight Q8501 and incidents known as "aircraft upsets" in the skies involving Qantas (2008) and Malaysian Airlines (2005) on-board computers.

Behind the story of the sophisticated fly-by-wire aircraft and the erosion of piloting skills, there is a worrisome sense that a huge industry now embracing the ideology of automation is needlessly putting human lives at risk by experimenting with technical innovations on commercial aircraft.

CHAPTER 1

–

AIR FRANCE FLIGHT 447
GOES DOWN IN
THE ATLANTIC OCEAN

May 31, 2009: It's 8 o'clock at night in Rio de Janeiro as the Air France Airbus 330-200 rolls down the runway at Galeão International Airport, following a half-hour delay. Among the more than 200 passengers flying to Paris are French nationals – business executives as well as tourists – and quite a lot of Brazilians, mostly students and some honeymooning couples eager to visit the old continent.

In addition, there are a variety of other nationalities and professionals from all walks of life: an opera director, a leading AIDS researcher, the head of the French-Brazilian Chamber of Commerce and even Pedro Luis de Orléans e Bragança, a prince who traced his lineage to the last Brazilian emperor. All had shared hugs and goodbyes with families and friends before embarking on what was to be a long, routine overnight flight to Europe. After dinner was served, the lights were dimmed and most of the passengers prepared to sleep as the Airbus crossed the ocean.

In the cockpit are three pilots: Captain Marc Dubois accompanied by co-pilots David Robert and Pierre-Cédric Bonin, referred to as First Officers. According to protocol, there are always at least two pilots in an Airbus 330-200 cockpit: One flies the plane, the so-called Pilot Flying (see Glossary page 186), the other (officially The Pilot Not Flying) manages communication and navigation, but can take command if necessary. This is done by using a button on the side-stick, which has replaced the traditional yoke on the Airbus. Behind the two pilots, there is a smaller seat – the jump seat – for a third pilot who can observe and assist his two colleagues from there. The Airbus 330-200 can readily be flown by two pilots, but a third is a welcome back-up for long stretches. Often in practice, the three pilots take turns.

The plane takes off in Rio and after gaining altitude and cruise speed First Officer Robert leaves his seat to take a nap in the cubbyhole behind the cockpit. A chime will awaken him when he is needed. It's business as usual for the crew. The route the aircraft follows from Rio to Paris is standard, the exact same route most airlines take when flying from South America's Atlantic Coast to Europe. The Airbus 330 will follow the Brazilian coastline to the northeastern city of Recife. From there, the aircraft will turn northeast away from the continent and begin crossing the Atlantic toward West Africa. Its last contact with "civilization" before doing so is the Fernando de Noronha archipelago off the Brazilian coast. From this point, the plane loses radar contact until coming into range of the Dakar radar in Senegal.

At 01:30 UTC (Coordinated Universal Time, a time standard that coincides with the time in the UK; Brazil is three hours behind - see Glossary page 191), the crew of Air France 447 makes contact with the final Brazilian radar station, Atlántico. They are told to remain at 35,000 feet.

"Wilco," says Captain Dubois, which means "will comply." "Thank you," replies the radio operator. Co-pilot Bonin is feeling uneasy after hearing over the radio that there is a storm ahead. He asks the captain: "We're not going to wait too long to ask for a higher altitude?" Dubois responds affirmatively, but takes no action nor does he ask Atlántico for higher cruising altitude.

A few hours later, Flight 447 has left the continental plate and is now coming in range of the so-called Intertropical Convergence Zone (ITCZ) (see Glossary page 185), a region around the equator infamous for storms and turbulence. These storms originate with warm humid air around the equator that surges upward upon colliding with the so-called eastern trade winds from the northern and southern hemisphere. The results are high-altitude thunderstorms. Unlike continental cloud formations that seldom rise higher than 35,000 feet, the ITCZ thunderstorms can reach 60,000 feet.

This means aircraft (with maximum flying altitude of 40,000 feet) have little choice but to fly through such storms. At night, with no visibility, the pilots must identify the storms by radar: Sometimes a crew tries to fly around the thunderstorm, others simply fly through it, avoiding the darkest parts and the heaviest turbulence. On May 31, Air France 447 was followed by another Air France plane, Flight 459, whose pilots decided to veer left sharply, successfully finding a path around the storm.

First Officer Bonin wants to fly higher, but Captain Dubois does not pay heed. The REC MAX or maximum altitude this plane was assigned to (this is dependent on weight, among other factors) is 37,000 feet. At this altitude, the plane is at its aerodynamic ceiling;

going higher would jeopardize its maneuverability. The captain clearly doesn't want to run this risk. He thinks everything will be fine, just like all the other times he's crossed the ocean.

Scanning the radar, Bonin sees the first storm front looming 200 miles ahead: "So, we have this thing here in front of us..."

The captain shrugs it off. "Yeah, I've seen it," he says.

The captain is flipping through a magazine. He starts chatting about tax havens. Bonin desperately tries to steer his superior's attention back to the storm. He remarks that they have just crossed the equator.

"OK, we'll take the necessary measures," Captain Dubois says nonchalantly.

Minutes later, the aircraft enters the clouds and Bonin switches on the landing lights to increase visibility. Some light bouncing begins. First Officer Bonin again: "It would be good to climb, wouldn't it?"

"When we get turbulence," the captain answers, alluding to more significant turbulence. They hear radio static. It's static electricity on the fuselage. Bonin believes they are near the top of the cloud canopy and weighs in: "Shouldn't we ask to go to 3-6 (36,000 feet). We're at the edge, even 3-6 would be OK." The captain again waves off the suggestion. "We'll wait until it passes." There's no reason to worry, muses Captain Dubois. He prepares to leave his seat to First Officer Robert who is returning from the cubbyhole and take a nap himself. Dubois gets a surprise though. A weird glow glances off the windshield, like a static electricity discharge. "Just what we need now... Mr. Elmo," the captain says sarcastically, referencing St. Elmo's fire, a phenomenon that occurs when it snows. But this doesn't keep him from leaving the cockpit. It is almost 01:50 hours. Co-pilot Bonin seems to believe everything will be OK. "I don't think the storm will be bad, not that bad," he says.

01:59:00

Dubois heads to the bunk as First Officer Robert takes the captain's seat on the left side, his colleague Bonin sitting on the right. Both pilots have a side stick to steer the plane, but only one is truly in control. The Pilot Flying is Pierre-Cédric Bonin. Bonin briefs his colleague about weather conditions: "The turbulence we just felt... we'll probably encounter more later."

02:06:00

Seven minutes later, Bonin briefs the purser on the Intercom, telling him to inform the passengers about turbulence ahead. Robert switches the monitor to Radar MAX, hoping to get a more accurate report on cloud formations. Robert does not have a good feeling. "You maybe want to go a bit left," he says cautiously. Bonin steers and the Airbus veers 12 degrees left of the original flight plan, but the aircraft is already smack in the middle of the storm. Both pilots hear the sound of hail hitting the fuselage. It gets hot in the cockpit and Bonin senses a strange smell.

"Anything wrong with the airco?" he asks, referring to the air conditioning. The more experienced Robert recognizes the smell. "It's ozone, nothing special. Just electrically charged air."

02:10:00

Just then, both pilots are confronted with the first incident that will unloose an uncontrollable chain of events.

The Automatic Pilot disengages and the Indicated Airspeed on the monitor falls from 274 knots to 55 knots (315 mph to 63 mph). Fifty-five knots is an unrealistic speed for this flight phase. The pilots know they must fly manually. Bonin alerts his colleague. "I have the controls."

What happened? The speedometers, or pitot tubes, have gotten clogged with ice in the storm and the Automatic Pilot has determined the given speed is being measured inaccurately and therefore disengages. This is not a problem in and of itself, because an A330 can be flown manually. But another consequence of the failing speedometers is that the flight status has changed from Normal Law to Alternate Law 2.

When flight status reverts to Alternate Law 2, normal "protections" of a standard flight are canceled. When an Airbus is in a normal flight situation, or Normal Law, the flight computers prevent the pilot from performing certain maneuvers like flying too fast or pitching too high. The so-called protections are turned off when the external inputs become uncertain or invalid – i.e. flight degradation occurs. The computers switch the flight status to Alternate Law 2 and the pilot must fly the plane with limited protections (the complete manual mode is called Direct Law), potentially putting the plane's aerodynamic limits at risk.

02:10:05

Not only has the Automatic Pilot disconnected, but also basic information on the Primary Flight Display – a digital screen where critical parameters such as altitude, speed and artificial horizon are displayed together – has disappeared. According to the Flight Display, vertical speed (gaining or losing altitude - see Glossary page 191) is increasing as the plane falls 1,000 feet per minute. At the same time, the Flight Director (see Glossary page 184) – a flight instrument overlaid on the attitude (see Glossary page 181) indicator that shows the pilot the pitch attitude required to follow a certain trajectory – has disappeared.

02:10:07

The Pilot Flying reacts by climbing. Bonin pulls the side stick backward, the nose pitches up from 0 to 6 degrees and increases throttle. At the same time, Bonin tries to control the roll caused by the turbulence. The Pilot Flying is overreacting – maybe it's nerves? – yanking first left then right on the side stick.

02:10:11

Seconds later, the Flight Director appears again (for only 4 seconds), recommending cruise altitude. Three seconds later, Bonin increases pitch – up 12 degrees – and the aircraft gains altitude more rapidly, 6,000 feet per minute.

The plane is now climbing too fast and too high, approaching 36,000 feet, but the crew is unaware. The Flight Director switches off again.

02:10:27

The Flight Director appears again and suggests maintaining vertical speed. Bonin's colleague, Robert, interrupts for the first time, telling Bonin to watch his speed. "OK, OK," Bonin says. "I'm going down again."

02:10:32

Barely half a minute has passed since the pitot tubes became clogged and the system disengaged.

Bonin pitches down slightly, 10 degrees above horizon (instead of 12 degrees) but this does not stop the plane from climbing. The plane passes 37,000 feet.

"You have to stabilize," Robert tells Bonin.

"Yeah," Bonin replies.

"You have to go down. This says you're going up. According to all three, you're climbing. Go down again."

02:10:47

The Flight Director reappears, this time for a minute, and indicates that the pilot must continue the climb rate, maintaining a vertical speed of 1,400 feet per minute. Bonin pulls back the side stick again, the plane pitches up 13 degrees above horizon. The plane is close to a stall.

The Angle of Attack (see Glossary page 180) – or relative position of the wings to the incoming airflow – has become so high that the plane loses lift and starts to fall. At that moment, First Officer Robert calls Captain Dubois on the intercom. Dubois is asleep in his bunk. "Damn," Robert says, "Where is he?"

02:10:51

At this point, the maximum vertical speed of Flight 447 has been reached. Because of the constant side stick inputs, pitch has increased 16 percent. The stall alarm goes off. In the cockpit, the first stall indications appear. The aircraft is buffeted noticeably as it loses lift. Then the plane rolls left to right.

Bonin increases throttle and pushes the levers to maximum thrust, or TOGA (Take Off Go Around – is the thrust needed for a plane to either Take Off or to gain altitude rapidly after an aborted landing, a so-called Go Around - see Glossary page 190) Increased thrust can serve as stall-avoidance since a plane needs a minimum speed to create lift. At this high altitude, Air France 447 has reached its power limit and the Angle of Attack has become extremely high due to continuous nose-up inputs. At this altitude, the only way to increase lift and avoid stall is to pitch down or lower the nose of the aircraft, but the pilots are overwhelmed with contradictory information.

02:11:12

The stall alarm goes off again. "What the hell is happening," asks First Officer Robert. "We have the engines, don't we?"

Robert is confused. The engines are working perfectly, but he thinks the stall is due to lack of speed, while it is actually an Angle of Attack problem.

Bonin pulls the side stick backward (nose-up attitude), but the machine is still in a stall. The plane reaches maximum altitude – 38,000 feet. In the 72 seconds since the pitot tubes froze and the Automatic Pilot disconnected, the Airbus 330 has climbed more than 3,000 feet.

Actual speed now is 183 knots or 210 miles per hour, correctly displayed on their Primary Flight Displays and the stand-by instruments, but it's unlikely the pilots are aware of this. They don't trust their instruments.

02:11:22

The aircraft begins to descend. Suddenly it lurches to the right and Bonin tries to counter, with little success.

"Do you know what is happening?" asks Robert. "Do you have any idea?"

"I've lost control of the machine," Bonin answers.

The situation is worsening. The plane descends at a rate of 10,000 feet per minute. At the same time, the aircraft rolls heavily left to right, the pitch varying between 11 and 19 degrees (the Angle of Attack has reached an improbable 40 percent whereas an Angle of Attack of 20 percent is already too much). The captain enters the cockpit. Although the stall alarm has stopped, the plane is still falling at a high speed.

"What are you doing?" demands Captain Dubois. "I don't know what's happening," First Officer Robert answers with disarming honesty. "We lost all control of the aircraft."

02:11:47

The pilots lower the pitch a little from 15 degrees to 11 degrees and put the engines in idle. Again the stall warning sounds. "I have the feeling we're flying at some crazy speed," says Bonin. He suggests slowing down and deploying the speed brakes, but Robert dissents.

02:12:10

Flight speed increases again. One of the two (either Bonin or Robert) understands they are flying too slow and moves the thrust levers to climb and then later to TOGA. But this has no effect. The plane fails to escape the stall situation.

02:12:44

The plane has descended to 20,000 feet. In 30 seconds, it will be below 10,000 feet. "We're there, we're there. We are going below level 100," says Bonin, using pilot lingo for 10,000 feet. The pilots recognize from the altimeter reading that they are descending. Outside it is still pitch black.

In this moment of crisis, Robert – perhaps because he is the more experienced pilot – believes he has to take over. "Wait, wait. I have the controls," he announces. Just then, a synthetic voice is heard: "Dual input." On an Airbus 330, both pilots can provide valid inputs with their side stick at the same time. Robert realizes Bonin did not release his side stick.

Still, none of the pilots know what is happening: "How come we are still descending?" asks Bonin.

02:13:36

"We are going below 9,000 feet!" screams Bonin.

"Climb, climb, climb," says Robert, as if he were talking to the plane.

"But I have been full back stick for a while," Bonin says.

When Bonin says this, Robert and Dubois seem to realize that Bonin had pitched up too much. Robert pushes his side stick forward as Captain Dubois yells: "Don't climb, don't climb." Again the synthetic voice: "Dual input, dual input." This suggests Bonin did not release the side stick.

"Go down then," orders Robert, alluding to what the captain said.

Robert pushes his side stick forward and air speed slows from TOGA to Climb Power setting, but again the synthetic voice sounds: "Dual input."

Because of the chaos in the cockpit and all the alarms going off, it is not clear who is flying. There is even less consensus about what should be done.

What's clear now is that First Officer Robert (supported by Captain Dubois behind him, or because he knows Bonin has pitched up too much?) wants to take control of the aircraft.

"OK, OK, you have the controls," Bonin says, then perhaps realizing he made a mistake and wants to compensate, adds "but careful, we are still in TOGA, eh."

There is a moment of lucidity. For the first time, the pilots make the right decision and pitch down, but it's too late. The nose is lowered 7 degrees under horizon; the speedometers appear again but another stall warning sounds. The confusion in the cockpit deepens.

Bonin pulls his side stick aft again, pitching up, setting off the "Dual input" warning. The captain, sitting in the jump seat, warns Bonin: "Watch out, you are pitching up again." "We have to," Bonin responds. "We are at 4,000 feet."

02:14:14

The Ground Proximity Warning System (GPWS - see Glossary page 185) springs to life. "Sink rate, sink rate." The machine is about to crash onto the surface of the ocean.

"Come on, pull up," urges the captain. "Come on, pull up, pull up!" says Bonin with urgency. The thrust levers go back to TOGA as both pilots pull back on their side sticks, producing a 16-degree pitch-up. In a normal situation, this would be enough for take-off. But the machine is in a stall. It is too late. "What's happening?" says Bonin, his final words.

02:14:28

Four-and-a-half minutes after the Automatic Pilot disconnected, the A330 crashes into the Atlantic Ocean with a vertical descending speed of 123 miles per hour. None of the passengers or crew survives.

An France Airbus 330 in flight. (photo: Air France)

Vertical stabilizer or fin of the wreck floating in the sea.
(photo: Brazilian Air Force)

Brazilian Air Force officer scanning for wreckage. (photo: Brazilian Air Force)

Brazilian soldiers stow the vertical stabilizer on deck of a navy ship. (photo: Brazilian Air Force)

CHAPTER 2

–

THE DOUBTS AND
THE CULPRITS

After Air France 447 went down, it took a long time – too much time – before the alarms bells went off in Paris. It was almost 5 o'clock UTC, when the Air France Control Center in Paris asked the Senegalese controller if he had had any contact with the aircraft. Neither Dakar nor the controllers at Atlántico had heard from the plane. Finally, in the early hours of June 1, Air France personnel tried to contact Flight 447 via relay calls (communication between planes) and satellite phone... to no avail.

Twenty minutes after the phone call between Paris and Dakar, the plane was officially reported as missing, but it wasn't until 09:20 before the first emergency call was sent out by control centers in Madrid and Dakar. At 11:00, nine hours after the crash, a plane took off from Brazil to search for the missing Airbus. Even if there had been survivors, help would have arrived too late.

The loss of the Airbus 330 above the Atlantic Ocean caused bewilderment, particularly in Paris. An Air France representative met with desperate family members who were still waiting for their loved ones at Charles De Gaulle Airport. Air France said it had no information to share. The plane had simply "disappeared" above the ocean; the airline suggested it could have been affected by the storm. Speculation that the plane had been hit by lightning was mentioned. Before noon, the "delayed" status of Air France 447 was removed. Air France CEO Pierre-Henri Gourgeon declared: "We are in the presence of a major air disaster. There is no hope at all of finding any survivors."

MEANWHILE, BACK IN RIO...

"We heard the news on TV," recalled Nelson Marinho, a retired Brazilian army officer. "I was sitting in my kitchen at 10 o'clock, when my wife called, and said: "Come quick, the TV is saying there has been an accident with an Air France plane." "From that moment on, we prayed. We knew Nelson Jr. was on an Air France flight – maybe even on the missing flight. He was flying on business to Africa with a stopover in Paris. But for a long time I hoped that he had survived."

I interviewed Marinho in his austere residence in Recreio dos Bandeirantes, a Rio de Janeiro suburb, in March 2015. Judging by the cleanliness of the place, Marinho is an orderly man. He is brawny and sports a military-style haircut. Marinho is pugnacious, serious and suspicious. During our conversation, it becomes clear that, in spite of the years that have passed – including a dozen or so flights to and from Paris and Frankfurt – innumerable meetings with family members organizations, lawyers and journalists, Marinho hasn't processed what happened. He hasn't said goodbye to Nelson Jr. His wife conveys a more melancholy figure. She sits down and talks about how Junior left behind a pregnant girlfriend who has severed all contact with the Marinho family. They rarely see their grandson. Nelson Sr. also has two daughters who live in Paris of all places, giving him another reason to travel there. His military background is further evident in his resoluteness.

"In the days after the accident, family members of the victims were invited by Air France to stay at the Windsor Hotel in Barra de Tijuca," Marinho recalls. Barra de Tijuca is a posh suburb of Rio de Janeiro not far from Marinho's house in Recreio. "People came from all around the country, there were more than 80 Brazilians on board Flight 447. We were briefed and given the latest news about the operation, the recovery of bodies, the search for the black boxes... There was free food and coffee, but we didn't get any answers to our questions about what had happened and most importantly: why...

"At a certain point, I stood up and said that everybody who wasn't satisfied with how Air France was treating the family members should get together and create an organization. The Air France employees looked astonished. They approached me and asked what I wanted, basically telling me to shut up."

Marinho refused to back down and the Association of Air France Flight 447 Victims' Family Members (AFVV447) was born.[1] The primary purpose of the organization founded by Marinho was to monitor the search and salvage operation, but it also sought to negotiate the financial compensation paid out by Air France and its insurance company AXA. Most of all, Marinho and other family members wanted to know the truth about what had happened on Flight 447.

---

1. The full name in Portuguese is *Associação dos Familiares das Vítimas do Vôo 447* (www.afvv447.org)

SEARCH AND RECOVERY OPERATION

In early June 2009, the Brazilian Navy started salvage operations at the last known position of the plane, namely near the Fernando de Noronha archipelago. Within five days, a Brazilian ship encountered a vertical stabilizer, or fin, with the Air France logo. It was floating near the Peter and Paul Islands, another 625 kilometers (388 miles) northeast of Fernando de Noronha. The site is roughly about 1,000 kilometers off the Brazilian coast and 100 kilometers north of the equator.

The fin was hoisted out of the water. It was believed that the entirety of the wreck would be recovered in a matter of days. Over the next several days, 50 bodies were recovered, among them that of the captain (who at the time of the crash did not have his seatbelt on), four flight stewards and 45 passengers. More than 1,000 pieces of debris were found and taken to the closest Brazilian city, Recife.

But after these early finds, nothing else was found and searchers realized the black boxes had sunk to the bottom of the ocean. The search wasn't going to be easy. The fuselage of the Airbus had sunk in an area comparable to an underwater mountain range, with peaks and valleys alternating from 800 to 4,000 meters. Black boxes emit clear signals for a month, but get weaker after that. After four costly salvage operations – three in June-August 2009 and a fourth in March 2010 – the search was called off. Although 6,300 square kilometers were searched up until that point neither the full wreck nor the black boxes were located.

CONJECTURE AND THEORIES

Notwithstanding the absence of the black boxes, soon after the crash theories and rumors began to circulate. There was early talk of a bombing, though this was rapidly discarded since the airplane had apparently hit the water in one piece. The latter deduction was based on the type of debris recovered and the way the fin appeared to have been ripped off. It was known that the plane flew through a storm, based on information from other planes flying near Flight 447. Air France itself had basic information on the flight's variables through the automated Aircraft Communications Addressing and Reporting System (ACARS – see Glossary page 178), which automatically reports maintenance-related info to airline headquarters via short wave radio and satellite.

From the ACARS messages, Air France and Airbus were able to deduce that the Automatic Pilot had stopped working and speed measurement had become unreliable, suggesting that the pitot tubes were clogged. The fact that the plane climbed to 39,000 feet also pointed to a stall situation. Was human error involved? Why would the pilots have climbed so high and put the plane at risk?

Soon enough, French and English tabloids began to leak stories alleging that the pilots had behaved irresponsibly in Rio the night before the flight. Reportedly, Captain Dubois and his girlfriend (an off duty air hostess and opera singer) had been out late with First Officer Bonin and his wife. They flew around the *A cidade maravilhosa* (The Marvelous City) in a helicopter and partied all night. Newspaper articles alleged that Dubois had slept only one hour before getting in the cockpit. However, it is common for a captain on long flights to be in charge for take-off then retire to the bunk and sleep, taking over again to control the landing. Take-off and landing are the only maneuvers done manually (though not always) while the Automatic Pilot controls the cruising flight. In addition, both first officers had plenty of experience and flight hours to pilot an Airbus 330 by themselves.

The media eagerly investigated how a modern sophisticated plane could have entered a stall without blatant human error being the cause. Before the official report was released, the BBC and the American popular science TV program NOVA had interviewed aviation specialists who questioned why the pitot tubes stopped working if an anti-freeze system was in place. The programs, which aired a year after the crash, speculated that the pitot tubes were clogged by liquid snow, known as "*greipel*".

The resulting lack of speed could have confused the pilots and they might have increased thrust and thus pitched up too much. But why would they have pitched up the aircraft? What really happened in the cockpit? To answer that question, it would be necessary to listen to the Cockpit Voice Recorder, which was lying somewhere on the bottom of the ocean.

THE BLACK BOXES

In Spring 2011, the non-stop pressure from Nelson Marinho and the AFVV447 had prompted a fifth search operation. This one proved successful. On April 2, almost two years after the crash, the black boxes were miraculously located. The point of departure for this search was the area from which Air France 447 sent out its final position in an ACARS message: 2°59' latitude (just north of the equator) and 30°59' longitude (in the middle of the Atlantic Ocean). This search was limited to a circumference of 37 kilometers. State-of-the-art technology was utilized and a mini-submarine belonging to Woods Hole, the U.S. company responsible for finding the wreck of the Titanic, located the remains of the fuselage. The remains of 104 passengers still strapped into their seats were recovered by divers and the black boxes were brought to the surface.

Despite the unexpected success of the operation, AFVV447 insists protocol was violated. Only Air France and Airbus personnel were present during the recovery of the wreckage and the black boxes even though both were directly involved in the crash. Marinho told me that the German group Geomar participated in the search but was not permitted to take part in the actual salvage operation. Against the wishes of AFVV477, the French Bureau for Investigation and Analysis for Civil Aviation Security (BEA) took charge of the black boxes. "From the beginning, things were all wrong with regard to jurisdiction," says Marinho, the former military man. "The plane crashed in Brazilian territorial waters, but the French led the salvage operation.

"Brazilians found the first parts of the wreck, but the French moved in right away and even stationed a warship in the area. After the black boxes were located, they were transported by nuclear submarine from French Guyana to France. This is illegal."

Marinho is right. According to international law, the investigation into an airplane accident should be carried out in the country where the accident took place. "We quickly understood there were powerful interests at stake, especially for France," said Marinho. "Both Air France and Airbus are more than companies, they are state interests."

Despite these irregularities, the Flight Data Recorder (FDR - see Glossary page 182) and the Cockpit Voice Recorder (CVR - see Glossary page 182) that make up the orange "black box" were downloaded on May 16, 2011, in the BEA offices in Le Bourget, near Paris. Aviation officials from Brazil, Germany and the United States (i.e., the National Transportation Safety Board, or NTSB) were present. The data from the black boxes would be used to reconstruct everything that happened leading up to the fatal final four minutes of the flight. However, it wasn't until July 2012 that the BEA finally published its official findings about the accident. The investigators concluded that the pilots lost control of the aircraft after the Automatic Pilot disengaged and they flew it into a stall.

The 230-page BEA report summarizes the events leading up to the crash, beginning with the failure of the Automatic Pilot forcing the pilots to take over. They reacted by pitching up too much, the report found, such that the plane achieved an Angle of Attack of more than 30 degrees. Flight 447 slowed to a dangerous speed and the plane began to fall. The report asserted that the pilots did not know how to regain control over the airplane, essentially declaring the cause of the crash to be pilot error. Although the BEA report identified mitigating circumstances ("... erroneous speed indications and the Electronic Centralized Aircraft Monitor messages did not help with the diagnosis. The crew became progressively destructured.")[2], it clearly blames the pilots without questioning the design concept of the plane, the fly-by-wire system or any inherent mechanical problems.

---

2. BEA report, p. 201 – Chapter 3: Conclusions

The investigation particularly cast doubt on the actions of First Officer Bonin, questioning why he repeatedly tried to pitch up even against the will of his co-pilot. They questioned why Bonin seemed obsessed with flying higher, suggesting he simply wanted to fly above the storm since he had asked the captain about that very possibility before Dubois headed to the bunk. Lead BEA investigator Alain Bouillard even argued later in an interview[3] that by pushing his side stick backward time and again "Bonin seemed to be curling instinctively into a fetal position."

Organizations supporting the victims' families in Brazil, France and Germany expressed skepticism as to the BEA findings and filed civil and criminal lawsuits in Brazilian and French courts[4]. Their primary legal accusation was that design flaws created the problem and the pilots were left trying to resolve them.

INCONSISTENCIES IN THE REPORT

Maarten Van Sluys did not accept the official version of the Air France 447 accident. He lost his sister Adriana in the 2009 tragedy. Van Sluys, a Brazilian of Dutch descent, works as a hotel manager. He spends much of his time travelling by plane around the fifth-largest country on Earth.

I talked with him via Skype in 2015. "My sister Adriana was a journalist," he told me. "So I decided to do what she would

---

3. William Langewiesche, Vanity Fair (The Human Factor, October 2014) http://www.vanityfair.com/news/business/2014/10/air-france-flight-447-crash
4. The French counterpart of *Brazilian Afvv447.org is Association d'entreaide et solidarité vol AF447* (www.association-af447.fr). The German organization is *Hinterbliebene der Opfer des Flugzeugabsturzes AF447*, or HIOPAF447 (www.hiop-af447.de)

have done, if I were on that plane. She would have started an investigation into the causes."

Van Sluys was among the first to respond to Nelson Marinho's call for family members to join forces.

"I was in the Hotel Windsor in Barra de Tijuca the week after the accident when Nelson invited all of us to form a group. He hosted the first meeting at his house; there were only a handful of us. But after a couple of weeks, his garage was full." Eventually Van Sluys took charge of the AFVV447 and its members have reached out to counsel family members of victims of other plane crashes, including the infamous Flight MH370 that disappeared over the South China Sea in 2014. Van Sluys' job requires a lot of air travel and he has become quite inquisitive about aviation. "Every time I board a plane, I ask the pilots and flight commanders questions," he said. "I look around a lot, I try to understand everything, how things work."

Though he spends a significant amount of time in the air, Van Sluys swears he's not overly concerned.

"I'm not scared at all. I think flying is very safe," he insisted. "In spite of the problems that do occur, flying has become safer and computers certainly have something to do with that.

"There is something based completely on logic in it. When there are two sets of data and a third is different, the computer avoids the one that is different." Another feature on these modern planes is that all systems are redundant, Van Sluys points out, so if there's a failure on one computer, there's a back-up, or even two back-ups.

"One could ask, 'How many tragedies have the onboard computers already prevented?' We don't know. The human element could be more dangerous than the computers. But history tells us computers also cause crashes."

Does Van Sluys really believe the Air France 447 accident was caused by computers? "Sure," he said. "I'm convinced of it. The famous pitot tubes malfunctioned and the computer sent out incorrect commands. The computer caused a hell of a mess in the cockpit and the pilots were completely betrayed by the machine.

"You could also ask, as does the BEA report, that after the pitot tubes stopped working and speed readings became unreliable, did the pilots react inappropriately?"

"Twenty years ago, a pitot tube might have frozen and the pilots simply would have kept flying. I've spoken with a lot of pilots and they say they are constantly trained in simulators and the bottom line is always *'You must trust your screen!'* That's what the instructors say over and over again: *'Rely on your instruments'*. But on the Airbus, the instruments were wrong. They displayed inaccurate readings about altitude and vertical speed."

CLOGGED PITOT TUBES: A NEW PHENOMENON?

"The obstruction of the pitot probes by ice crystals at cruising speed was a phenomenon well known but misunderstood by the aviation community at the time of the accident," concludes the BEA report[5].

This is most decidedly not true. Defective pitot tubes, false speed readings and the strange effects these erroneous readings can cause for onboard computers were not unknown in 2009.

---

5. BEA final report on the June 1, 2009, accident (published in July 2012): Chapter 3.2 - Causes of the accident, page 201.

It seems readily apparent that these events were occurring more often than was made public. Such incidents still occur, but do not always have the fatal consequences seen in the Air France accident.

Pitot probes are small tubes attached to the fuselage that record incoming air pressure. The Indicated Air Speed of a plane is calculated by subtracting the atmospheric pressure from the airspeed measured by the pitot tubes. Indicated Air Speed is an indispensable element for flying for which there is no real alternative, not even a GPS.

The role the faulty pitot tubes played in contributing to the crash cannot be underestimated and the report's attempt to explain it away as a "misunderstood phenomenon" did not go unnoticed. An organization created by family members of the French victims of the AF447 crash places special emphasis on the faulty pitot tubes in the lawsuit it filed against Air France and Airbus. The group – known as *Association d'entreaide et solidarité AF447*, or asso447 – is expecting a verdict in 2019. Their legal case places special emphasis on the faulty speedometers made by French manufacturer Thales, arguing that the airline and the aircraft constructor must be held legally responsible.

Laurent Lamy, a freelance computer programmer from Orléans, is the French counterpart of Nelson Marinho and Maarten Van Sluys in Brazil. Lamy – who lost his brother Eric on the fatal flight – and his mother Danièle preside asso447. Lamy has conducted his own investigation and he has become somewhat of an expert on pitot tubes, especially the Thales AA probes that were installed on all Airbus 330s. There is evidence that they were known to have performance issues in cold temperatures.

"Air France and Airbus knew for a long time that these pitot tubes were not working well," Lamy told me in a Skype interview in March 2015. "But they failed to take any preventative measures." For the pitot tubes to work at high altitude, where temperatures reach -50 degrees Celsius (-58 degrees F), a heating system is supposed to keep the pitot tubes working properly. The heating system in the newer models of Thales pitot tubes was flawed.

The first Airbus 330-200 aircraft was flown in 1998 and the problem with the heating system in the pitot tubes was first detected in 2008, Lamy told me. During the Airbus 330's first decade aloft, the older models of pitot tubes apparently did not generate major problems.

"It is striking that between 2003 and 2007, there were only nine reported problems with frozen Thales AA pitot tubes on Airbus 330 aircraft," Lamy said, quoting the counterexpertise[6] presented in a Paris courtroom in a criminal case against Airbus. "Beginning in 2008, these events increased spectacularly with 16 occurrences that year alone and 10 more during the first few months of 2009. It is possible that a change was made in the heating system of the Thales AA tubes and it didn't work very well."

Among the Airbus pilots and crew working at Air France, this problem did not go unnoticed. In early 2009, an internal directive ordered that all model AA Thales pitot tubes be replaced by June 2009.

"The replacement (of the faulty pitot tubes) on the Airbus that was Flight 447 was programmed upon its arrival in Paris!" Lamy said. It is significant that Air France had diagnosed a

---

6. The counterexpertise is based on BEA reports handed over to Judge Emmanuelle Robinson of the Higher Court in Paris on Feb. 13, 2017.

critical failure on its Airbus 330 fleet but did not ground the planes and replace the faulty parts. There were five months between the replacement order and the maintenance job scheduled for the doomed plane.

WARNING SIGNS IGNORED?

Lamy told me about other cases involving frozen pitot tubes on Airbus 330 models. "Ten days before the Air France 447 accident – on May 21, 2009 – the Brazilian company TAM had a flight from Miami to Sao Paulo during which the Thales AA pitot tubes froze, leading to the loss of all air speed reference data and the disengagement of the Automatic Pilot and the Auto Thrust (see Glossary page 181)," he said. Airspeed and altitude information was lost and the plane went from Normal Law to Alternate Law. This is basically the same thing that happened on Air France 447. "But after resetting the computers and relying on their stand-by instruments, the pilots were able to fly on," he told me.

TAM Flight JJ8091 was investigated by the U.S. National Transportation Safety Board (NTSB) since the flight took off from the United States. After an investigation of more than two years ending in July 2011, the NTSB concluded that "a brief and temporary blockage of the pitot probes in cruise flight, most likely due to ice crystals aloft, led to erroneous airspeed indications and airplane automation degradation." According to the NTSB "contributing to the incidents were design features of the Thales AA probes which left them more susceptible to high altitude ice crystal icing, than other approved pitot probe designs."

That the problems resulting from failing pitot tubes on Flight 447 was not an isolated case is further illustrated by another episode around the same time as reported by the website *The Aviation Herald*, a website that tracks civilian aviation incidents.

On June 23, 2009 – three weeks after the Air France disaster – an Airbus 330 owned by Northwest Airlines flying from Hong Kong to Tokyo gave the pilots a major scare.

"In an area of cirrus clouds, the Automatic Pilot and Auto Thrust disconnected, the crew lost all speed and altitude references and the machine went into Alternate Law until the end of the flight," *The Aviation Herald* reported. In this case, the pilot acted in similar fashion to the pilot on TAM Flight JJ8091 a month earlier. "He kept his composure and flew at recommended thrust of 83 percent of capacity and recommended pitch, flying the plane out of the cloud zone. The fly-by-wire remained in Alternate Law for the rest of the flight," wrote *The Aviation Herald*. After this event, Delta Airlines (which had acquired Northwest eight months earlier) replaced all pitot tubes on their A330s.

Lamy mentioned a few additional cases. "In August and September 2008, the year before the Air France 447 accident, there were two near-crashes with Airbus 330-types owned by Air Caraïbes Atlantique, flying from Paris to Martinique. In these incidents, the same freezing of the speed sensors in a high-altitude storm caused a degradation of flight parameters," he said.

Fortunately, disaster was avoided. The problem, according to Lamy, is not the failing speedometers in and of themselves, but the way the flight controls suddenly suffer degradation. A false reading is misinterpreted by the onboard computers, which then make erroneous conclusions that produce faulty commands.

---

7. June 23, 2009. http://avherald.com/h?article=41bb9740&opt=0

After a lengthy fight against industrial giants Air France, Airbus and BEA, Lamy has lost faith in the French justice system. On the asso447 website, the most recent post is dated March 2014. That final post reviews a directive issued by the European Air Safety Agency, or EASA (similar to the airworthiness directives sent out by the FAA) that forbade the use of Thales AA pitot tubes on all planes using European airspace. In a second interview in March 2015, Lamy told me this EASA directive clearly places the blame for the crash retroactively on Airbus. "By prohibiting the use of Thales AA pitot tubes, the EASA implicitly admitted that loss of air speed measurement is extremely dangerous on those automated planes."

But no tougher measures have been taken against Airbus or Air France by authorities despite this damning conclusion. No officials from Airbus or Air France have faced charges for the Air France 447 crash. According to aviation lawyer Marc Fribourg who advises the French families' organization, "in France it is impossible to win a verdict against the aircraft constructor Airbus. The planes are treated as if they have no defects."

In June 2016, Fribourg's law firm won a small victory when a judge issued a provisional ruling that Airbus and its insurance company Artus were responsible for a crash that occurred with AirAsia Q8501 (See Chapter 4). "That is unprecedented in French justice," he said.

Lamy is obviously frustrated and exasperated. When I later asked if his brother had been in Brazil on business or on vacation, he answered curtly: "It doesn't really matter if he were on holiday or on a business trip... or where he lived. He is dead now. Sorry, I'm being a bit blunt."

TRUST YOUR INSTRUMENTS... SOMETIMES

Laurent Lamy's Brazilian counterpart, Maarten Van Sluys, says a pilot is trained "to always trust his instruments." But the clogged pitot tubes on Air France 447 not only disengaged the Automatic Pilot (a good thing, taking into account the unreliable speed readings), they also led to erroneous information on the dashboard Primary Flight Display.

At 02:10:05 UTC, when the Auto Pilot disengaged, the Primary Flight Display indicated the plane had lost 1,000 feet and was descending at a vertical speed of 600 feet per minute. It is not clear whether Bonin's reaction to this imaginary descent, pulling his side stick back to climb, was a reaction to this misinformation. But because of the mantra constantly drilled into pilots' heads – "always trust your instruments" – it appears to be an appropriate reaction. What can't be denied is that there clearly was a serious glitch in the computer software on the Airbus 330. If the Automatic Pilot disconnected due to an unreliable speed reading, why didn't other instruments – like the Flight Director – reject the unreliable speed readings and erroneous altitude calculations?

In fact, the French BEA concluded that there was something wrong with the instruments, in particular the Flight Director. A Flight Director is a flight instrument that shows the pilot the attitude required to follow a certain trajectory. The crossbars of the Flight Director represent the position of the plane and its wings on an artificial horizon. "When an unreliable airspeed event occurs, the automatic control features (Auto Pilot and Auto Thrust) disconnected automatically. The crew could only then re-engage them by pressing on a dedicated push-button...

The Flight Directors behaved differently," the BEA stated on page 190 of its report.

At 02:10:05 the crossbars of the Flight Director had disappeared, but two seconds later they reappeared, suggesting the need to climb. The BEA report continues: "The credibility of the crossbars is strengthened by their disappearance followed by their reappearance: If they are visible, it implies the indications on display are valid. Since they attract the crew's attention (a green presentation in the center of the Primary Flight Display), the presence of the crossbars could have influenced the actions of the Pilot Flying, notably in respect to his reaction (to ignore) the stall warning."

"Flight Director Indications that may have led the crew to believe their actions were appropriate.... One may therefore question the suitability of the automatic appearance of the Flight Directors once they have disappeared."

The BEA is suggesting that the onboard computers should not be programmed to automatically re-engage the Flight Directors when doubt remains as to their reliability. But the BEA's conclusions are abstract, legalistic and confounding. The phrase "One therefore may question the suitability of the automatic appearance of the Flight Directors once they have disappeared" is a rather dispassionate assessment of a critical software error on the Airbus 330.

Another BEA conclusion: "The underlying behavioral hypotheses in classifying the loss of airspeed information as 'major' were not validated in the context of this accident. Confirmation of this classification thus supposes additional work on operational feedback that would enable improvements where required, in crew training, the ergonomics of information supplied to them and the design of procedures."

Not really a ready-made set of instructions for pilots.

THE FAULTY ALARMS

On forums and blogs one can find a lot of criticism about how the Air France pilots handled the plane after the Automatic Pilot disengaged. What perplexes many is why the pilots did not react properly to the stall warnings that sounded in the cockpit. Were they simply overwhelmed? Did they believe the stall warning was incorrect? Was Bonin convinced they were actually in a high-speed stall? ("It looks like we are flying at some crazy speed," he was heard to say.)

Was Bonin applying the wrong protocol? This is a possibility since Bonin followed the unreliable speed protocol for low altitudes (increase pitch and thrust) suggesting he might have been confused. We must also not forget that the Airbus 330 was touted as a plane that would never stall and that most Airbus pilots will never have to apply stall recovery in their lifetime. But here again, the stall alarm was flawed and this confused the pilots.

After the disengagement of the Automatic Pilot handed the controls over to the pilots, the stall alarm sounded briefly at 02:10:11, but did not sound again until 02:10:54. By then, the airplane had already entered into a stall and the situation was beyond critical. Why wasn't the stall alarm working and why was it triggered when the pilots were making the necessary decisions to pull out of the stall?

Airbus 330 pilot Bill Palmer who wrote a book about the technical details of the crash ("Understanding Air France 447") knows why the stall alarm wasn't working. "The stall alarm is triggered by the Angle of Attack sensors," he explained in his book. "There are three sensors and, unlike the pitot tubes that measure speed, these weather-vane like devices on the side of the plane measure the angle of the airflow relative to the airplane fuselage and the wings." Palmer points out that the Airbus stall alarm does not work at low speeds. "The design logic is that the airflow must be sufficient to ensure a valid measurement by the Angle of Attack sensors."

Former RAF fighter and B747 captain Alastair Rosenschein supports Palmer's explanation. "On the Airbus, the stall alarm does not work below 60 knots," he told me in December 2016. "It is designed like that. If not, the stall alarm would be going off all the time when the plane is on the ground as the wind can play around with the Angle of Attack sensors."

"On a Boeing, there is another device that recognizes when a plane is on the ground, so the stall alarm is never inhibited," Rosenschein said. "The Airbus stall warning system is, in my opinion, an important design flaw on those planes." In other words, on the Airbus 330 (and similar models) the stall alarm is disabled when the plane flies slower than 60 knots. That is a serious problem, because a low-speed stall occurs at... well... low speeds.

According to Palmer, the speed of Air France 447 never fell below 60 knots, so even according to Airbus logic, the stall alarm shouldn't have been inhibited. But the stall alarm was not working because the plane *seemed* to be flying slower than 60 knots due to "the outright blockage of the pitot tubes by ice crystals."

When the pitot tubes unfroze a minute later – as the airplane started to descend – the pitot tubes still could not record the real speed because "the Angle of Attack was so high the pitot static system could not effectively measure the forward airspeed," Palmer wrote.

For the pilots on Flight 447, the situation was very confusing. At one point during those four fateful minutes, they made the right decision to lower pitch by reducing thrust (thrust was set into idle at 02:11:47). But the stall alarm went off again! Palmer explained: "The decreased pitch reduced the Angle of Attack slightly, which was enough to push the indicated airspeed up to about 80 knots, revalidating the Angle of Attack information and activating the stall warning again."

But the ill-fated pilots could not have been expected to understand this amid the chaos. Former Air France pilot Gerard Arnoux, a technical advisor to the victims' families in their legal proceedings against Airbus and Air France in Paris, joined Rosenschein in criticizing the counter-intuitive stall warning. "*Un avertissement à contre sens*," he calls it in his native French.

"This stall alarm violates the European Certification for Large Aeroplanes, issued by EASA in September 2007," Arnoux wrote me in December 2016. Article CS 20.207 specifies that a stall alarm "must be furnished by a device that will give clearly distinguishable indications under expected conditions."[8]

Arnoux believes the most important system breakdown that fateful night over the Atlantic was the lack of a warning that

---

8. EASA, Certification Specifications for Large Aeroplanes CS-25, Sept. 19, 2007, p. 1B-21: https://www.easa.europa.eu/system/files/dfu/CS-25_Amdt%203_19.09.07_Consolidated%20version.pdf

the pitot tubes were clogged. Such information would have alerted the pilots to the unreliable speed readings. "Normally there would have been an alarm on the ECAM (Electronic Centralized Aircraft Monitor - see Glossary page 183) urging the pilots to check their speed and apply the proper protocol for unreliable speed.

"In other known cases where the pitots became clogged, the ECAM alarm worked, enabling the pilots to start the procedure of unreliable Indicated Air Speed, which is described in the manuals," Arnoux said.

"This breakdown of the ECAM system on Flight 447 put the crew in a situation where they were forced to improvise instead of carrying out objective troubleshooting. There was nothing in the manual about how to react for what happened during those four minutes."

FIGHTING AIRBUS IN COURT?

One of the beneficiaries of Arnoux's counter-expertise against the BEA report is Maarten Van Sluys. The Brazilian hotel manager is adamant that financial compensation is not a motivation. He insists his only desire is to establish the truth about Flight 447.

"We don't expect a resolution for 10 or 12 years, by 2020," van Sluys said. "It took 12 years to resolve the Concorde lawsuit (following the July 25, 2000, crash). We are very anxious to see that final judgment, which certainly will not match the BEA report."

Van Sluys believes the big aircraft constructors simply refuse to recognize errors with the construction of their planes. In contrast, automobile manufacturers are occasionally forced to recall certain models due to design flaws. "We're talking about big money here. The replacement of Thales pitot tubes by a Goodrich model, for example, costs $90,000 each. That's $270,000 dollars per plane," he said. The recall of computer parts would also be prohibitively expensive, added Van Sluys, suggesting that the airlines and aircraft manufacturers simply couldn't afford these costs.

"But I think there's another reason," he continued. "Recalling airplanes is an admission that there is something wrong with the design concept and Airbus has put all this effort and money into promoting a fully automated airplane."

Van Sluys further argued that the plan to operate planes without pilots in the near future is another key factor in the legal battle. "Those people… will never admit that there are flaws. In fact, pilots that fly those machines say they don't feel very comfortable, because they know they are not totally in charge.

"Nowadays, pilots are just button-pushers. The software designers say: 'You have been given the best software in the world. If you don't do anything, everything runs smoothly. Don't interrupt anything the computer is doing…' that is, until the computer stops working."

There's an interesting man-machine paradox in what Van Sluys is saying. Onboard computers were introduced to prevent human error. But when the computers fail, that same "untrustworthy" pilot must then serve as a back-up to the failing computer. So do we need another computer to control the "failing pilot"? It's a paradox reminiscent of Joseph Heller's Catch-22 – coincidentally set in the world of aviation.

Nelson Marinho with a picture of his deceased son. (photo: Reuters)

The Van Sluys Family: Maarten and his deceased sister in the middle. (photo: MVS)

Cockpit of an Airbus 340 with Primary Flight Displays of pilot and co-pilot. (photo: Venancio Ozino)

◻ The lack of a clear display in the cockpit of the airspeed ··· ·
  by the computers;
◻ The crew not taking into account the stall warning, which could have been due to:
  • A failure to identify the aural warning, due to low exposure time in training to stall phenomena, stall warnings and buffet,
  • The appearance at the beginning of the event of transient warnings that could be considered as spurious,
  • The absence of any visual information to confirm the approach-to-stall after the loss of the limit speeds,
  • The possible confusion with an overspeed situation in which buffet is also considered as a symptom,
  • Flight Director indications that may led the crew to believe that their actions were appropriate, even though they were not,
  • The difficulty in recognizing and understanding the implications of a reconfiguration in alternate law with no angle of attack protection.

Excerpt of the BEA report on the malfunctioning Flight Director on the A330. (photo: BEA)

	2003	2004	2005	2006	2007	2008	2009 (8 premiers mois)	Total 2003 à août 2009
quantité globale	1	2	1	4	4	18	18	48
Pitot AA	1	2	1	4	1	16	10	35
Pitot BA	0	0	0	0	0	1	4	5
goodrich	0	0	0	0	0	0	3	3
Pitot non déterminé	0	0	0	0	3	1	1	5

BEA Chart (in French) about faulty pitot tubes (incidents from 2003 until 2009), used in the case before the French criminal court. (chart: BEA)

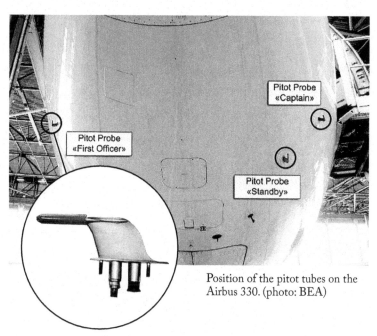

Pitot Probe «Captain»

Pitot Probe «First Officer»

Pitot Probe «Standby»

Position of the pitot tubes on the Airbus 330. (photo: BEA)

The infamous Thales AA pitot tube with flawed heating system.

CHAPTER 3

—

HABSHEIM AND
THE AFTERMATH

The fatal flight of AF447 may have been the biggest air disaster involving Airbus and Air France, but it definitely wasn't the first incident involving computers and fly-by-wire. These incidents date to the late 1980s when fly-by-wire was first introduced in civil aviation.

Tragic accidents including Bangalore (1990), Mont Sainte Odile (1992), Toulouse (1994) and Habsheim (1988) cast serious doubt on the commercial future and safety of this advanced technology in passenger transportation.

Airbus was the first company to fully embrace and promote fly-by-wire. It's interesting to consider how the rise of Airbus tracked the gradual incorporation of fly-by-wire in passenger aircraft.

THE COMPETITIVE EDGE

Airbus was just 15 years old in the mid-80s, a small but ambitious player competing against giants in the aviation industry, like Boeing and McDonnell Douglas. Airbus was a true European company, born in 1970 from the fusion between French Aerospatiale, German Airbus and British Hawker Siddeley (Aerospace). Later on, Dutch Fokker, German Messerschmitt and Spanish Casa would join the venture. Although Airbus' first planes – the A300 and A310 – enjoyed decent sales, Airbus executives understood they needed something new to wrest market share away from the big American competitors. And the new technological breakthrough would come, as has often happened before, from military aviation.

On fighter planes, fly-by-wire (i.e., electronic command of airplane controls) had gradually replaced the old system of cables, pulleys and levers. The evolution provided enormous advantages, especially with regard to weight as the old cable system (often redundant for security reasons) depended heavily on hydraulics.

Less weight meant less fuel and lower operational costs. Computers also make flying more "intelligent," less complicated and more user-friendly. A variety of orders can be given at the same time and they can be calculated in relationship to external factors. For instance when flying in turbulence, the computer can compensate for certain inputs to make a flight more comfortable.

Among the key features of fly-by-wire are the built-in protections: This means a pilot is prevented from exceeding the aerodynamic limits of the plane such as maximum speed or stall angle when these protections are in place. For military aircraft, these protections provide huge benefits because they allow the planes to stretch their capacity to their maximum. The human factor, the chance of pilot error in navigation or handling of the controls, is reduced and in the rare case of a computer error, there is always the ejection chair.

In the early 80s, there was a man in France who believed this technology could be transferred perfectly to civil aviation. Bernard Ziegler was the vice president for engineering at Airbus and the son of the former company CEO, Henri Ziegler. Before rising in the ranks at Airbus, Bernard Ziegler had been a student at the famed École Polytechnique and had enjoyed a prolific career as a fighter pilot. He fought in Algeria and was twice decorated. After his military career, he flew as a test pilot, first for French Dassault and later for Airbus. Due to his experience as an engineer and a pilot, Ziegler became the most important promoter of fly-by-wire, seeing it as a means to make the planes more efficient.

THE BIRTH OF THE A320

The first Airbus equipped with this technology was introduced in 1987. The A320 aroused great expectations in the public and across the airline industry. More than 400 pre-orders were received before the first machine was airborne (in comparison, when an earlier Airbus-model – the A300 – was launched in 1972, only 15 pre-orders were placed). The strongest objection to the new technology wasn't the safety of crew and passengers, but the expectation that the computers would produce massive lay-offs. In fact, one of the features of the A320 was that the traditional trio of pilot, co-pilot and flight engineer was replaced by a different trio: pilot, co-pilot and... *the computer.*

This decision didn't go over well in France where national airlines Air France and Air Inter were the obvious A320 customers. The airlines were controlled by the same politicians who controlled Airbus. The French national pilots union (SNPL), active in all the national airlines, promptly went on strike to oppose the purchase of the new Airbus models. The SNPL union was sure the new plane would gradually remove the engineer from the cockpit. The union was right. "This machine can be piloted by my *concièrge*," Bernard Ziegler had declared somewhat arrogantly at the launch of the A320. What he had meant as a pithy phrase to emphasize the blend of user-friendliness over the sophistication of the machine came across as a stated preference for automation over manpower.

The union protests and strikes did not dampen the enthusiasm and expectations for "this marvel of technology" and on Feb. 22, 1987, at 9.30 a.m., the first A320 took off on its inaugural flight from Toulouse (the home of Airbus) in the presence of Prince Charles and Princess Diana.

The flight was glitch-free and the British, German and French crew described it as the "most pleasant, smooth and silent machine" they had ever flown.

A year later, when the first A320 purchased by Air France was presented to the public, the media were ecstatic. The plane (with serial number F-GFKA) made a low flight over the Champs Elysées with its spiritual father Bernard Ziegler and Prime Minister Jacques Chirac on board. The crowd cheered as the plane flew low over Paris then descended for its landing at Charles de Gaulle Airport. As the machine rested on the tarmac, Michel Asseline, an Air France captain heading the A320 test pilot division, noticed the flaps were not retracted. He asked pilots Hilaire de Malglaive and Robert Merloz if anything had gone wrong. Asseline recalled that both pilots looked pale and stressed. They confessed that they had experienced breakdowns and failures of important instruments during the flight, the most significant being a malfunction of the 28-volt transformer that feeds direct current to elementary functions on the plane. The switch to the back-up transformer hadn't worked and the pilots said they were at the point of losing both their instruments and their electrical commands. Fortunately they were able to rely on a battery that provided just enough power to land but not enough to retract the flaps. The much-lauded electronic plane had been close to a major disaster… ironically because of the lack of electrical current.

At the time, Asseline chose not to reveal anything about these problems to the public. "We wanted to show the aircraft at its best," he wrote three years later in his book *Is the pilot to blame?* We had blind belief in the Airbus technicians who assured us that these were just growing pains," Asseline wrote. "We were proud to participate in this great adventure that would lead the European aircraft industry to its rightful place in the world."

As the European aircraft builders struggled to increase market share, they actually found a key ally in the United States. The software that controlled the so-called flying laws of the A320 was originally conceived by NASA for the Space Shuttle. Actually, the normal flying law of the Airbus 320 – known as C^* (verbalized as c star) – is also used on the F-16 and is based on a load factor of G1 and zero roll. This means that while in cruise attitude, the amount of lift will equal gravity and the plane will always look for this aerodynamic stability. The software acts on the controls to find the right balance (G1). It is a simple concept shared by the early Airbus collaborators including Asseline, who defended the plane patriotically.

In this spirit of loyalty, Asseline ignored other malfunctions that appeared through early 1988 while he and a select crew of Air France pilots tested the plane. Asseline did not realize until later that the A320 had been pushed too early into use for commercial reasons without sufficient testing. "There were some parts of the plane that hadn't been certified when Air France started operating it," he admitted. For example, there were problems with the altimeter, the evacuation system and the retraction of the landing gear. "The biggest challenge for certification lay in the software of the plane, and because of intellectual property rights, the code was never disclosed to certifying authorities," wrote Asseline.

Asseline confessed that he "did not sleep, nor did he have a family life" in 1988, because he was so obsessed with guaranteeing the success of this new machine. In June of that year, he was asked to fly a short demonstration flight from the city of Mulhouse. This flight was programmed for Sunday, June 26. Asseline did not hesitate to accept and he sacrificed another Sunday that could have been spent with his family. "I wasn't particularly keen on this sort of work, but it seemed to be a good means to promote the A320 and its extraordinary possibilities."

THE MINISTER'S AIDE

While Captain Asseline prepared for the next day's demonstration flight, a married couple and an Air France pilot were enjoying dinner in a chic Paris neighborhood. Norbert Jacquet – a Boeing 747 (Jumbo Jet) pilot – was a longtime friend of Dominique Ruffieux. Her husband was Jean Francois Gueulette, a close advisor to French Transportation Minister Louis Mermaz. Jacquet had served as a witness at their marriage. Spirits were high as the three opened a costly bottle of Medoc and the conversation turned to the controversy caused by the A320 in the French aviation industry.

Jacquet said he thought French airlines were "moving too fast," reminding his dinner guests that neither Air France nor Air Inter[9] had experienced any major accident in 20 years. "They will have accidents with the A320," Jacquet said twice, hoping Gueulette would take his concerns to Minister Mermaz. Jacquet told them of comments and experiences other pilots had shared, even offering to talk to the transportation minister himself.

The next day Jacquet flew out of Charles de Gaulle Airport (Roissy) in the cockpit of a Jumbo 747 cargo plane, headed to Koeweit City with a stopover in Pakistan. He was focused on his plans to go crab fishing the next day. In an odd twist of fate, Jacquet's future would be intrinsically entwined with that of another plane passing over an air show at the very same moment he was taking off.

THE AIR SHOW DISASTER

Air France Flight 296, an Airbus 320, had taken off from the French airport of Mulhouse in the Vosges forest near the conjunction of the French, Swiss and German borders. There were more than 100 passengers on board, all having bought tickets for this demonstration flight hosted by the Air France commercial service. The flight plan included flying over the Alps, including Europe's highest mountain, Mont Blanc, before descending back to Mulhouse. Right after take-off, the A320 was to do a short fly-over at the nearby local aerodrome of Habsheim, only 10 kilometers from Mulhouse.

---

9. Air Inter was a regional airline which later merged with Air France.

The local flying club was eager for the new Airbus – this new wonder of technology – to parade a few minutes past its enchanted visitors mingling among all the classical biplanes. The spectators watched in awe as the huge plane descended, took a turn and flew over the short 1,000-meter runway only 30 feet above the ground with its landing gear out and its nose in a sharp pitch-up maneuver. This posture was quite unusual for a commercial airplane. They watched as the Airbus passed by the control tower, approaching a small forest that borders the end of the runway. While everyone waited for the plane to gain altitude, the aircraft clipped the tops of the trees in the forest and disappeared. After a few seconds of silence, a huge column of smoke rose from among the trees. The public looked on in shock. The A320 had crashed!

It took some time for Captain Michel Asseline to realize what had happened after the plane came to a stop a few hundred meters into the thick forest. The tail of the plane and the back of the fuselage had shaved the top of the trees, and then the right engine had caught fire. Toxic smoke was seeping into the plane, but the evacuation protocol – the alarms, synthetic voice with safety instructions, and exit lights on the floor – was not working, so evacuation was slow and chaotic. One of the stewards pushed open the front exit door, but it got stuck and opened only halfway. The evacuation slide inflated inside the plane. Thanks to the heroic effort of four air hostesses, most of the passengers were helped to safety. The pilot, a former rugby player, was able to lift his unconscious co-pilot Pierre Mazières from his seat and drag him out of the plane. Unfortunately three passengers died: a woman who tried in vain to rescue a child but succumbed to the toxic fumes herself, and a third passenger, a disabled boy, who was stuck in his seat. Most of the passengers, as well as the crew, were transported to a nearby hospital.

As the news of the crash reached Paris, the political world in France reacted in shock: an accident with an Air France plane! The company had a spotless reputation and its new Airbus 320 was touted as a technological marvel. This disgrace could quickly become a commercial disaster, with 400 A320s being built in Toulouse for their respective customers. French Transportation Minister Mermaz acted quickly to dispel any doubt about the plane, declaring that *"l'avion n'est pas en cause"* ("the machine should not be questioned"), indirectly passing the blame onto the pilots. This was quite premature, since the black boxes had yet to be recovered and an official investigation had not even started. The passengers and crew were still in a hospital in Mulhouse when Norbert Jacquet, in the Far East, heard about the crash on the radio.

"I was sad at first, but also relieved in some way that there were only three people to mourn," Jaquet said. "Usually in air crashes we hear about dozens or hundreds of victims." He naturally thought of the prescient conversation he had about the accident-prone A320 with his friends the night before he left Paris. He also thought it was quite unusual that the pilot had survived, so Jacquet was anxious to talk to him and to hear, first-hand, what had happened.

Back in Paris a few days later, Jacquet found an interesting message on his answering machine: It was his friend Dominique congratulating him on his clairvoyance and mentioning the Metz accident (mistaking Mulhouse for Metz, a city in the same region). "Your words have been confirmed by the facts," she said, "things have gone too far." Jacquet interpreted the message to mean the Gueulettes wanted to talk to him about the case. He returned the call to ask how the news of the crash had been received by the transportation minister. Jacquet immediately noticed that his friend sounded aloof, speaking uncomfortably. When Jacquet said he expected more from her, Dominique responded: "But you know as well as I, Norbert, that we have to take into account the collective interests."

This suspicious silence had the opposite effect on Jacquet. He followed the coverage of Flight 296 closely, worried that the traditional SNPL appeared to be toeing the Air France line too slavishly. He promptly decided to establish an independent pilots union. Together with his colleague Yves Stéphan, Jacquet founded the Air France Airline Pilots Union (SPLAF, in French) on June 30, 1988, only four days after the Habsheim crash. In their first communiqué, the pilots attacked the board of Air France for uncritically protecting the interests of Airbus, also a national company: "Air France doesn't have any respect for its 35,000 employees, their pilots and their crew, all of whom could become victims of a failing security policy."

TOO LOW, TOO SLOW?

Jacquet wondered about the cause of the accident. Fed by suspicions of the plane's airworthiness, he watched the amateur footage available from the fateful air show with more than the usual attention. It was aired on French national television the same day of the accident. The footage sparked considerable speculation about why the A320 did not pitch up in time before it plowed into the woods.

The official version that the pilot apparently "flew too low, too slow and pitched up too late" was considered ludicrous by the SPLAF and Jacquet offered this argument a few days after its release: "Supposedly this accident was the fault of the pilot, but this would be quite surprising: This man was in charge of teaching his colleagues at Air France, perhaps forcing us to conclude that the other pilots he trained are worth less than zero."

"Pilot error hasn't been proven at all. On the contrary, the authorities revealed that the engines were at full throttle at the time of the crash, but the plane descended. Strange. Supposedly the computer prevented a stall situation and thereby saved the lives of most of the passengers. But wasn't it the computer that, by limiting the action of the pilot, actually caused the accident?"

It would appear logical that Jacquet and Asseline would be natural allies, since Jacquet defended the Habsheim pilots against the authorities who sought to make him the fall guy. But oddly enough, after Asseline was released from the hospital and had an hour-long conversation with Jacquet, the Flight 296 pilot refused to criticize the aircraft at all.

"It's a very good machine," Asseline said. "She has to fly. One should not touch it."

"But you are in the middle of it," Jacquet said.

"I am not important," Asseline replied. "What counts is the A320."

Jacquet concluded that his colleague, who at that time was "being dragged through the mud by French officials and Airbus," was either being manipulated by his pride, or "he has made a deal with the authorities to cover up the plane's problems."

Asseline admitted in his book that investigation commission members – some of whom were close colleagues, including

Boeing 747 Captain Claude Béchet – were initially very nice to him and his co-pilot Mazières. But "this sweet-talking approach changed as soon as I asked to see the listings containing the details of the flight."

Two months after the accident, Asseline was forced to appear in front of a disciplinary committee. He eventually had his license revoked.

The pilot changed his opinion with regard to the plane and refused to cooperate with the committee. Ten years later, he was convicted and sentenced to 18 months in prison, though he only served nine months.

CONTROVERSY AND COVER-UP

Captain Asseline himself described the months after the crash as a traumatic wake-up call. He gradually began to remember clearly that, before reaching the forest, he did activate the throttle levers, but the engines simply did not react. Moreover, as time passed, Asseline became more and more convinced that French authorities – from the transportation minister to Airbus company officials and Air France executives – were carrying out a cover-up.

All the blame was being placed on him in order to whitewash the plane's role in the crash. Asseline now believes – as does Jacquet – that the cockpit voice recordings and the listings of the Flight Data Recorder were tampered with and they do not correspond to the real flight parameters. Asseline also believes the black boxes presented in court are not the ones rescued from the plane.

The pressure on fellow pilot Jacquet got steadily worse. He was a *cavalier seul* (a lone ranger) taking on giants – Air France, Airbus Industries and Francois Mitterrand's Transportation

Ministry. Jacquet received threatening phone calls, he was being followed on the street by undercover police officers and he lost his job at Air France because of "psychological problems." He was even arrested, taken to a police precinct and sent to a psychiatric hospital for observation. Asseline would later describe this persecution of his colleague as "worthy of a (communist) Eastern European regime."

Jacquet was cleared by the psychiatrist who said he hadn't found anything abnormal, but his career as an Air France pilot was over, despite strike action organized on his behalf by the SNPL union. He went bankrupt and was forced to sell all of his belongings. He ended up living "like a *clochard* on the street." Due to his persistent criticism, Jacquet was barred from flying in French territory and, on top of that, he was later sued by new Transportation Minister Michel Delebarre for slander. Delebarre succeeded Mermaz, the man who defended the A320 after Habsheim only to resign two days later, in essence accepting the political responsibility for the disaster.

THE BLACK BOXES OF FLIGHT 296

In July 1988, after Jacquet's explosive declarations, there emerged across France a public debate over whether this was pilot error or if there was evidence that something was wrong with the A320. French and English television programs (especially British Channel Four) questioned the new fly-by-wire technology and the safety of the A320. In addition, irregularities in the recovery and analysis of the black boxes triggered legal action.

The night after the crash, the black boxes were flown by Transport Minister Mermaz to Paris and dropped off at the national Test Fly Centre (CEV) in Bretigny, a suburb south of

Paris. The CEV is part of the Transportation Ministry whose public declarations had already defended the airplane, so it was not exactly an independent and objective arbiter.

On June 30, Judge Mme Marchionni ordered the handover of the black box to Justice, but the order was ignored. On July 5, another judge, Germain Sengelin, issued a capture order for the black boxes. When Judge Sengelin was informed that the Cockpit Voice Recorder was being held by the Civil Aviation Directory in Paris, he ordered the black boxes be seized.

Upon arriving in Paris, the policemen sent by Sengelin were told the black box was stored in a locker for which nobody had the key. The following day – July 6 – the Cockpit Voice Recorder was finally handed over to Justice, after having been in the possession of the Transportation Ministry for 11 days. Critics, including Jacquet, are convinced this time was used to alter the AF296 flight parameter listings. Whether the listings were altered or not, the subject was debated in French courts for the next 10 years. Asseline's defenders insist the listings were altered to hide the A320's anomalies and to place the blame on the pilot.

WHO WAS TO BLAME FOR THE HABSHEIM ACCIDENT?

As Asseline himself admits in his autobiography, he had never really been in favor of touristic flights for PR purposes, but on that fateful Sunday he was also careless in his preparations. Doing a fly-over at an air show with passengers on board is against the rules. Although the decision was made by the marketing arm of Air France, the ultimate responsibility lies with the pilot who accepted the mission. The flight was especially risky, because it was to be done at "a high Angle of Attack." Asseline had told his co-pilot Mazières the day before the flight that they would fly over with a high pitch-up attitude to impress the bystanders at the air show. Mazières agreed. This was a predictable choice, since the attractive feature of the A320 was exactly that: Its extraordinary ability to fly at this high Angle of Attack without stalling. Asseline would never have done this with any other plane, without the built-in protections.

In addition, the maps of the region provided by Air France were not entirely accurate. Asseline had no idea there was a forest beyond the runway. Ultimately, Asseline was perfectly aware there were bugs in the new software in the A320 but he ignored this, apparently thinking these were minor problems he could work around. After all, he was a big fan of the new plane. Until it crashed.

THE ALTIMETER BUG

A serious bug on these first A320s involved one of the two altimeters (see glossary page 179).

When Asseline received the plane the night before from his colleague Captain Chatelain who had flown in from Berlin, his colleague told him "the *barometric* altimeter setting did not provide real values." The barometric altimeter displayed erroneous data, like the altitude of the airport at take-off: this altimeter bug would appear after switching on the new digital navigation system, a feature of the A320 that generated computer animated images of airport destinations and how to approach them. After the Habsheim accident, Airbus admitted in its Operational Engineering Bulletin OEB 06/2 that a bug in the altimeter did indeed exist. The bulletin reported that incorrect altitude readings could be displayed after "*the disconnection of the Auto Pilot or electrical transitionals,*" whatever that meant.

Asseline wasn't surprised by what Capt. Chatelain told him as he received the plane on the 25th of June. He had experienced the same problem with the barometric altimeter settings while flying from Paris to Geneva a month earlier on another A320 that had been delivered to Air France.

On May 26, 1988, Asseline had approached Geneva at what he thought to be a safe altitude of 4,000 feet, when suddenly through a break in the clouds he saw he was flying too low over Lake Geneva. Upon landing, the altimeter read 1,000 feet instead of 0 feet. "We were lucky that day, God was with us," Asseline confessed. They had even flown over the Jura Mountains – which reach an altitude of 5,640 feet – with the erroneous altimeter setting.

A month later, even with the specific information that the barometric altimeter wasn't to be trusted, Asseline chose not to use the other altimeter at his disposition: the *radar* altimeter (see glossary page 179). Instead, he decided to trust the flawed barometric altimeter. "The A320 featured a new digital radar altimeter that presented numbers rather than a needle, which makes it harder to read," Asseline said in defending his decision not to have used the radar altimeter instead of the flawed barometric altimeter.

Coincidentally or not, the problems with Flight 296 originated with an erroneous altitude reading. Just a few minutes after the A320 had taken off in Mulhouse and as it was descending toward Habsheim, co-pilot Mazières noticed they were too low. "Watch out, you're approaching 100 feet," he warned his colleague upon seeing the altimeter indicated the plane was around 150 feet. In reality, the plane was already lower than 100 feet. The altimeter was wrong. When Mazières mentioned the reading, the plane was already flying below 50 feet. Too low! Not only hadn't they seen a visual warning on their navigation screen, the pilots were not aware of the audio warnings coming from the digital radar altimeter that was working properly.

As they flew over the aerodrome, both pilots saw the forest pop up at the end of the runway.

"This was not the mental scheme I had prepared for this flight," Asseline confessed afterward. "Instinctively, in a fraction of a second, I first put the thrust levers into idle and then into full throttle. I kept the plane horizontal and flew by sight. The forest got closer. Still no engine thrust. These seconds seemed like an eternity. My throat got dry and my heart was beating fast."

"TOGA," said co-pilot Mazières. "He was completely calm," Asseline remembered, "like in a simulator. Now we had thrust, I pulled the yoke. But the plane didn't follow my orders. The trees got closer..."

They crashed into the tops of the trees. Asseline described the sensation of the branches brushing across the windshield like being in a carwash. After the plane came to a stop, Mazières was unconscious. He opened his eyes shortly thereafter and said: "But what have you done?" Asseline answered: "I don't know. I don't understand."

DISCONNECTION OF THE AUTOTHROTTLE SYSTEM

After reliving the accident hundreds of times in his dreams as well as in a simulator, Asseline came to a conclusion about what went wrong. The engines responded way too late to the increased thrust and when he pulled the yoke, instead of climbing, the plane pitched down.

With regard to the first problem, Asseline argues that "there was a delay in the transmission of the order to the engines, due to a computer failure in the Auto Thrust system."

According to Asseline, the fly-by-wire on the A320 was to blame for this and some anomalies were already apparent at take-off. On the tarmac in Mulhouse, the principal computer on the plane (the FMGC) had told them to switch the thrust levers to CLB (Climb Position), a position used *after* take-off. But the machine was still on the ground! "He is asking us to CLIMB already, the idiot," Asseline recalled having said to his colleague.

Asseline believes there was a problem between the computer and the Automatic Thrust (AT) system and this problem could have produced the disengagement of the AT. On the A320, when the AT is disengaged, the thrust comes back only gradually. (Asseline quotes the Airbus 320 manual: "When the AT is disengaged or fails, the thrust is fixed in its current value. Then the levers should be moved from that position, after which the thrust will gradually evolve toward the position of the thrust levers.")

Asseline insists that was what happened to him while flying over Habsheim. The Autothrottle (see Glossary page 181) had disconnected, but the pilots were not apprised, he declared.

Later, after listening to the Cockpit Voice Recordings during the investigation into the crash, the A320 pilot actually heard the alarm sent out by the Flight Warning Computer (FWC), a chime sound announcing that the AT had shut off. "But among all the other sounds, we hadn't noticed," Asseline says. As the plane flew over the Habsheim aerodrome, the pilots did not know the AT was disengaged so could not calculate the effect this would have, specifically a critical delay in changing the thrust from idle to TOGA (Take Off/Go Around, or maximum speed)

Was the computer to blame for shutting down the AT or was the pilot to blame for not noticing it? It is not unusual for glitches and defects to appear in a new machine. On the other hand, as the head of the A320 division, Asseline was seemingly the best-placed man to deal with these flaws.

A variety of malfunctions linked to the fly-by-wire system (the computers) were apparent: problems with the barometric altimeter, lack of communication between the onboard computers, problems with a disconnecting AT. Nevertheless the machine was still deemed fit to fly, and it was certified by French and European authorities. In the United States, the certification process was still under way at the time of the Habsheim accident. The desire for approval from U.S. authorities presented a significant motive for the French Transportation Ministry to defend the aircraft.[10]

Asseline himself, the Airbus man who had defended the automated plane from critics and had made personal enemies of the cockpit engineers who were now out of a job, completely changed his opinion about the aircraft. After the accident he no longer was convinced of the benefits of fly-by-wire technology.

---

10. In October 1990, more than two years after Habsheim, the Delebarre Cabinet issued a communiqué announcing that the National Transportation Safety Board (NTSB, the U.S. transportation authority) had cooperated in the investigation of the accident. But on Dec. 17, the U.S. Federal Aviation Authority sent a letter to the Air France Union "denying that the NTSB has cooperated in any way with the Habsheim investigation." Two days later, Delebarre resigned as transportation minister.

THE ROOT OF THE SOFTWARE ERRORS ON THE A320

After his pilot license was revoked, Asseline got a lucky break. He was hired by Thomson Industries in November 1988. This construction giant made the simulators for Airbus and sought Asseline's experience as a tester for the A320 simulators. After having been suspended from Air France – the new job allowed him to take a critical look at the conception of the A320.

"One of the main problems with the new technology on the planes is the faulty interaction between different systems," Asseline wrote in his book.

For safety reasons, all computer systems are not only redundant (there's a back-up in place in case a system fails), they are also separated.

"The principle of separation means that each circuit controls a different function of the plane – tire pressure, air conditioning, cabin pressurizing, carburetor circuits, engines, brakes, etc. – so the failure of one circuit does not affect another," says Asseline. But this healthy firewall, so to say, did not apply to the diagnostic system.

"One problem on the A320 is how the Centralized Fault Display System (CFDS) works," says Asseline. "Here, all the separate computers are linked in the analysis of what's going well and what is not. So when there's a bug or if the system reports a failure when there is none, this error message will be taken into account by the CFDS as a real failure and affect the ongoing diagnosis of other functions."

Asseline recalls that in the early months of A320 testing, the computers would go haywire on the pilots. Asseline and Mazières did not comment on this publicly, but there were recurring events where the computers affected the controls. "On those first A320 test flights, the crews experienced sudden cabin depressurization after selecting more than four navigation modes!" Asseline says. "These depressurizations forced emergency landings. Apparently, the computer had concluded after selecting these different *Navaids* that the atmospheric pressure was 0."

Asseline remembers one test flight just a month before Habsheim (in May 1988) where there were multiple failures of the Automatic Pilot, the Auto Thrust and the Flight Director, and that these failures came from a faulty transmission from the flaps and slats. Asseline did what most people would do with a balky computer: Switch it off and on. "I resolved it by resetting the computers that control the flaps (SFCC1 and SFCC2) and everything went back to normal."

Asseline also cites a colleague, Claude Dalloz, who reported that on a Paris to Amsterdam flight in August 1988, two months after Habsheim, he got an alarm message warning that "only his trim tab" was working. This meant he had "lost" his tail elevator, the principal control for ascending or descending.

Other alarms popped up: "Fire in the toilets," "problems with the automatic pilot," and "problems with the landing gear." Dalloz decided he had to return to Paris and as a precaution he did a few flyovers so that the Paris airport controllers could visually confirm if the landing gear was out. Once confirmed they were out, he put the plane back on the ground in Paris.

Asseline says Dalloz "was not congratulated for a job well done – instead he was reprimanded – because Air France was sensitive about its public image, especially since (the incident) occurred so soon after Habsheim."

After serving out his sentence, Asseline moved to work in Australia. He is currently retired and living in the French province of Bretagne. He now wants nothing to do with airplanes or aviation. This contrasts with Norbert Jacquet who is frequently sought out for interviews by the French media every time there is an airplane accident.

JACQUET ALLEGES RECORD-TAMPERING

The former Jumbo pilot is now considered a madman by some, while others view him as fighter for truth. His book "The Assassin lives in the Elysée" is similar to Emile Zola's "J'accuse." In the style of the best French revolutionaries, he takes on the French authorities, Air France and Airbus. He believes they were involved in a conspiracy to absolve the A320 aircraft, because there were two much more deadly crashes after Habsheim: one in Mont St-Odile and one in Bangalore. In both cases, the fly-by-wire system came under suspicion.

The Mont St-Odile crash occurred near Strasbourg, not far from Habsheim and was blamed on a navigation error, apparently caused by, among other things, the fact that the automatically generated charts had been displaced. The pilots made a VHF Omnidirectional Range or so-called VOR approach (when there is insufficient visibility, this non-precision approach relies on the instruments) using the wrong latitude and crashed into a hill near the airport.

The Bangalore crash occurred during a descent when the pilots were unable to advance the throttles and the plane impacted the ground, then lifted up briefly before crashing on a golf course.

After criticizing the premature absolution of the A320 by

Transportation Minister Mermaz the day after the Habsheim crash, Jacquet became suspicious about how the investigation evolved. He called into question the integrity of the Béchet Commission, the official investigative body that looked into the Flight 296 crash. The commission examined two sources of evidence related to the events of June 26, 1988: The testimony of the pilots (a rare source after aircraft accidents) and the flight recorders, both the CVR and the FDR. As mentioned earlier, these recorders had been downloaded in Brétigny before the judge ordered that they be handed over.

On Aug. 18, the Béchet Commission published its conclusion. The report identifies a gap in the information, pointing out that some 10 seconds are missing just before the end of the recording. The commission explained this "gap" by arguing that "as the aircraft hit the trees, the cables of the recorders located close to the landing gear were damaged."

This explanation, insists Jacquet, is preposterous. "The cables run right underneath the fuselage and are reinforced to withstand the possible explosion of a tire," he argues. "In similar accidents, like the one in Bangalore when the aircraft hit the ground with a force of 6 Gs, the recorders kept on working. So why would they stop when the airplane lightly brushes the trees? And then why would they start again?"

Jacquet finds it very suspicious that this "gap" appears right at the time Capt. Asseline had switched the levers to full throttle: The listings, or read-outs, now suggested he had reacted too late.

More suspicious to Jacquet and Asseline is the lack of synchronization between the CVR and FDR timelines. As published in the Official Journal, there is a two-second inconsistency between the FDR and the CVR, taking as a point of reference the audio and digital warnings from the radar altimeter, "40 feet... 50 feet... 40 feet," that the plane was flying too low.

Jacquet thinks it's strange that these announcements didn't come with a standard time lapse between them, like synthetic voice announcements usually do. Actually in the first report the time lapse between the first and second announcements is 1.3 seconds, and the difference between the second and third announcements is 2.6 seconds. This suggests that the timeline was altered.

AN INCORRECT ANGLE OF ATTACK?

Even on the official (perhaps altered) listings published in the Official Journal, Jacquet finds reasonable proof that the plane did not react as it should have. Apart from the late reaction of the engines, there was the incorrect pitch-down of the A320, as Asseline pulled the yoke fully aft. "The official version is that the plane didn't react to Asseline's orders to pitch up, because the maximum Angle Of Attack (AOA - see Glossary page 180) had been reached (more than 17%)," Jaquet says. "But in the data provided by the Official Journal, the Angle of Attack was recorded as between 14% and 15%, so there was no reason for the computer to have limited the pitch-up order."

According to Jacquet, the AOA was even *lower* than 14%. After recalculating other variables such as the relationship between altitude, pitch and the distance the plane flew over the forest, Jacquet concluded that the real AOA when Asseline pulled the yoke was not more than 10%.

This percentage was later confirmed by Marcel Lejeune, a navigator who participated in the readings of the Flight Data Recorder. He also served as a prosecution witness in the libel and slander case Minister Delebarre filed against Jacquet and Asseline. "The case is very simple," Lejeune declared. "There are sectorial differences, but the real AOA in Habsheim was 10%."

So if there were no imminent danger of stalling, why would the plane have countermanded Asseline's orders?

Jacquet believes this happened because "the normal C* flying mode had been changed to the flare mode unbeknownst to the pilot. On the A320, the *flare mode* is automatically engaged when the radar altimeter indicates the plane is 100 feet above the ground. If the flare mode was engaged mistakenly (without the pilot's knowledge), the pilot would suddenly be dealing with new variables related to pitch and flying angles. A staunch critic of fly-by-wire, Jacquet refers to it as "*Une conception abracadabrante des commandes de vol.*" ("A voodoo-like conception of the flight controls.")

After his Habsheim experience, Captain Asseline has serious questions as well about the A320 landing law, the so-called flare mode. He says it is "nothing less than perverse" that it automatically engages at 50 feet. "First of all, it is engaged without informing the pilots," he points out. "The plane gradually – and automatically – pitches down -1.25 degrees per second under 30 feet, even without the intervention of the pilot."

"Once this *automatic flare* has started, there are only two ways this process can be stopped: by landing or by giving full throttle (TOGA). But as long as the speed hasn't increased, the pilot's pitch-up inputs will not be obeyed by the computer and the plane will only climb gradually." Asseline argued that the built-in protections on the A320 actually put the lives of the Habsheim passengers in danger instead of protecting them, because the aircraft can't gain altitude quickly when there's an obstacle on the runway.

To emphasize his point, Asseline cited another (non-fatal) A320 accident a year after Habsheim. In December 1989, there was a runway collision involving an A320 belonging to the French company Air Inter and a small Mooney airplane at the Lille airport. The Airbus pilots were landing in a thick fog when they suddenly saw the other plane on the runway. The pilots reported that the Airbus controls would not allow them to execute a *go around* (full throttle to take-off). The bigger plane slammed into the Mooney, spinning it across the runway. The Dutch pilot of the Mooney was lucky to survive. Just like at Habsheim, the automatic evacuations and public address system failed to work, a serious flaw on the early A320s. According to the BEA investigation, this was due to a *software error* in the Cabin Intercom Data Systems of the A320. This innocuous admission essentially means the BEA acknowledges the existence of software errors.

Asseline concluded that "it would have been much simpler if under 50 feet, the horizontal stabilizer controls are handed back to the pilots." With a hint of sarcasm, he says "that probably would have been too simple for the designers of this plane, who view the art of piloting to be negligible and prefer leaving the decision to computers." This overdependence on computer systems in modern aircraft is also bitterly criticized by Jacquet. He has made the conundrum of *pilot versus computer* his personal crusade. "A computer can never replace a man," he says. "Unlike a human being, a computer can't react to the unexpected. And in aviation, the unexpected is always a certainty."

Air France Airbus 320 before his first commercial flight, with fly-over in Habsheim. (photo: Pascal Van de Walle)

Passengers boarding Flight AF296 on June 26, 1988. (photo: Pascal Van de Walle)

Airbus 320 flying over Habsheim aerodrome at high Angle of Attack.
(photo: amateur footage)

Airbus hitting the top of the trees at the end of the runway.
(photo: amateur footage).

Minutes after the evacuation, the pilots -one of them with bloodstained shirt- are in disarray. (photo: Jean- Claude Boetsch)

Only the tail is left from the burning wreck of the A320. (photo: Jean-Claude Boetsch)

Pilot Michel Asseline shows
disbelief after the Habsheim crash.
(photo: Jean-Claude Boetsch)

Michel Asseline shows a picture
of the aircraft at a meeting with
passengers of Flight 296. (photo:
Jean-Claude Boetsch)

Air France Captain Norbert
Jacquet in a Boeing-cockpit
before Habsheim. (photo: NJ)

Airbus-critic Norbert Jacquet
during an interview, after the
AF447-crash. (photo: NJ)

CHAPTER 4

—

AIRASIA: A CRACKED SOLDER JOINT AND A DISASTER WAITING TO HAPPEN

If we are to believe the statistics, flying in commercial airplanes has on average become safer each and every year. Since the 1980s, air crash fatalities have decreased annually, in spite of the increased appetite for flying, which now sees 90,000 commercial flights daily across the globe.

Despite this trend toward ever-safer air travel, 2014 was a clear exception. That year was a black mark on aviation history with at least 21 fatal accidents and a death toll of 990 people, greatly exceeding the death toll of 2013, the safest year in commercial flight history (265 people died in airplane crashes that year while 1.25 million people were killed in road accidents that same year).

One could argue that the tragic year of 2014 is an exception to the tendency toward safer flight. After all, on the surface there doesn't seem to be any link between the accidents; the increase could be seen as mere coincidence.

In March, a Malaysian Airlines plane with 239 people on board, the MH370, disappeared off the radar above the southern Indian Ocean. The reason for its disappearance remains unknown. In July, another Malaysian Airlines jet, the MH17, was shot down above the civil war zone in Ukraine. That same month, there was a crash of a TransAsia plane in Taiwan and an Air Algérie plane went down in Mali.

One accident in particular gets our attention, the last one of that fateful year, the crash of an Airbus 320 belonging to low-cost airliner AirAsia. On Dec. 28, Flight 8501 took off from Indonesia headed to Singapore. It went into a stall and crashed into the Java Sea, killing more than 162 people. The AirAsia case bears frightening resemblances to the Air France 447 crash.

RUDDER PROBLEMS AND SUBSEQUENT STALL OF AIRASIA

On Dec. 28, 2014, most of the passengers on Flight Q8501 were traveling from Jakarta to Singapore. Many were foreign laborers headed back to work. The plane took off at 5:35 AM local time (22:35 Universal Time) for Singapore, and many of the 162 passengers were still half asleep.

Soon after take-off, the airplane cruised at 32,000 feet, flying over the Java Sea that stretches between Borneo and Java. Everything seemed to be going smoothly. The captain – Malaysian pilot Iriyanto – was monitoring the plane, while First Officer Rémi-Emmanuel Plesel, a French pilot, was actually flying the plane (dozens of French and European pilots are employed by Asian carriers because of job cuts at French and European airlines).

At 22:57 UTC (05:57 local time), the flight attendant told passengers to fasten their seat belts because of turbulence ahead. Three minutes later, at exactly 23:00 UTC, while the pilots studied the weather ahead, they received a warning on the Electronic Centralized Aircraft Monitoring, or ECAM, screen (warnings about technical problems are displayed on the ECAM screen as are the recommended steps to resolve them). The message read "AUTO FLT RUD TRV LIM SYS," identifying a problem with the "Rudder Travel Limiter Unit." This unit does not move the rudder itself, but it limits the range of the rudder movement. It is one of the famous "protections."

In the Airbus fly-by-wire system, the rudder is controlled by two *redundant* Flight Augmentation Computers (FACs) such that if one fails, the other takes over. The ECAM system not only warns of failures, but also recommends the action to be taken by the pilot. In this case, the suggestion was to reset the two FACs that control the Rudder Travel Limiter Units (RTLU - see Glossary page 189) by pushing buttons on the overhead panel. After that, both RTLUs returned to normal function, apparently.

Four minutes later, the captain who had been wary of heavy weather before this ECAM message came in (he was concerned about some cumulonimbus clouds), contacted the nearest controller asking permission to deviate the aircraft 15 miles to the west, heading for 310°. Flight Officer Plesel asked Iriyanto about looking for an alternate airport in case of an emergency. Both pilots likely considered the message about the rudder flaw as a potential problem.

At 23:09 UTC, another ECAM message again warned of a faulty RTLU, triggering a chime and a master caution light. The pilots repeated the ECAM action and again, both RTLUs were reported as returning to normal function.

The pilot immediately contacted Air Traffic Control (see Glossary page 179) in Jakarta to inform them the flight had turned left to avoid weather. The pilot also asked for permission to climb to 38,000 feet, but this request was denied (they were asked to stand by) because of other planes in that area. Then a third and fourth error message regarding the RTLU came across, and both were "resolved" in the same manner, by resetting. At 23:16 UTC, Jakarta controllers finally cleared the pilot to climb to 34,000 feet, but the pilot did not respond. Instead, his focus was on the ECAM screen.

A fifth error message had appeared as well as a sixth. They were completely different than the previous messages. This time the two FAC computers themselves seemed to be failing (AUTO FLT FAC 1 + 2 FAULT). As a result, the Auto Pilot and the Auto Thrust disengaged.

Flight control law reverted from Normal Law to Alternate Law and the protection envelope parameters were lost. Suddenly the aircraft rolled to the left at an extremely high 54-degree angle of bank. After the right side-stick was activated, the roll angle was reduced to 9 degrees left but then it rolled another 53 degrees left. Captain Iriyanto, sitting on the left hand side, was fighting to control the roll, while Plesel – on the right side – started a climb maneuver. The pilots pitched up and the aircraft climbed to nearly 38,000 feet (at an incredible climb rate of 11,000 feet per minute). At one point, around 23:17 UTC, the stall warning activated and continued until the end of the flight. The airplane was flying at a dangerously slow 140 knots and had entered into a stall. As the machine began to fall at a rate of 12,000 feet per minute, the Angle of Attack was almost constantly at more than 40%. The plane crashed into the Java Sea. No emergency message had been transmitted by the crew.

SALVAGING THE WRECKAGE AND THE OFFICIAL REPORT

Most of the passengers on board were Indonesian citizens. This was no coincidence since AirAsia – a former Malaysian national airline – is very popular in Indonesia. It had nearly gone bankrupt in the 1990s until flamboyant Malaysian businessman Anthony "Tony" Fernandes acquired it and transformed it into a popular low cost carrier in the fashion of Virgin, Jet Blue, Ryanair and Easy Jet.

According to Fernandes, more than 50% of his clients are first-time flyers, since flying used to be reserved for the elites in Southeast Asia. Then AirAsia began offering economical flights with the tagline: "Now everyone can fly." It is also interesting to note that AirAsia is the world's largest operator of the Airbus 320-200 with almost 200 of these aircraft types in its fleet. Having a single model in house makes it easier for pilots and maintenance crews. At least in theory.

As soon as Q8501 went down, there were reports from fishermen in central Kalimantan (Indonesia) who had seen a plane fall out of the sky. A large rescue operation involving Indonesian ships, helicopters and planes was undertaken as 2014 came to a close. Malaysia, Australia and Singapore joined the search. Even the United States and Russia provided logistical assistance to locate the wreckage.

On the first day of the New Year, debris was found floating in the Java Sea and on Jan. 7, divers found the tail of the aircraft in the water. Over the course of the next week, the fuselage was discovered, as were the CVR and the FDR (the black box) near the wreck on the sea floor.

By March 2015, all the larger pieces of the jet's fuselage had been recovered and hauled back to Jakarta for the investigation. It took the Indonesian Safety Board of Transportation (KNKT - see Glossary page 193) almost a year to publish its 206-page Accident Investigation report. The KNKT made it clear that its main purpose was "to promote aviation safety" and that it was not looking to "lay blame or liability" on anybody. The results of this investigation were published in a KNKT document.

Because they had recovered the biggest part of the fuselage, the safety board was able to dissect the rudder and the affected FACs and RTLUs. Investigators found that the reason for the fault messages on the ECAM was an electrical problem, an oxidized circuit. This was quite a revelation, since it meant a specific small technical problem was located on an underwater wreck, yet it had not been discovered above ground by the maintenance crew. It turned out that the mechanical (or computer-related) malfunction on this Airbus 320 had existed for quite some time but it had not been detected by maintenance. Or had it?

The KNKT report is quite distressing in this regard. It was not the first time the RTLU on this Airbus 320 had sent fault messages to the crew. At least four separate crews had issued Pilot Reports (or Pireps) about these RTLU fault messages on this plane in 2014 alone. According to protocol, these Pireps should have led to maintenance action and a maintenance report.

In the automated world of planes, pilots aren't required to fill out a report after leaving the cockpit. All malfunctions are recorded automatically. All the ECAM messages a pilot sees on his screen are recorded in a CFDS (Centralized Fault Display System) that prints out a Post Flight Report. This is reminiscent of the ISO-certification process wherein everything is documented though not necessarily resolved.

Airbus has two different kinds of Maintenance Reports: the MR1 and MR2. The MR2 is a secondary or deferred defect log book reserved for flaws not deemed urgent because they are not part of the Minimum Equipment List. When there are no spare parts available, these fixes can be postponed.

The MR2 defects should not affect airworthiness. For whatever reason, the RTLU defect was not addressed even though this specific problem with the RTLU of the AirAsia Airbus 320 had been recorded not once, but 23 times! The RTLU on the Flight Q8501 Airbus had been causing trouble roughly once a month until September 2014, after which the problems multiplied exponentially.

In December 2014 there were no fewer than nine RTLU incidents, the last one occurring on Christmas Day, three days before the fatal flight of Q8501. The pilot flying that Airbus 320 on Dec. 25 was Captain Iriyanto, the same pilot in command of Flight Q8501 on Dec. 28, a fact that is not without importance. The captain had been forced to deal with this exact problem before, so he might have become fed up with it.

Iriyanto dealt with the rudder limiter problem and the trouble shooting process for the first time on Christmas Day, and this would have an effect on the unorthodox way the aircraft was handled ahead of the fatal crash. Then, Iriyanto was preparing to take off from Surubaya Airport in Jakarta, Indonesia, en route to Kuala Lumpur, Malaysia, when the AUTO FLT RUD TRV LIM SYS message appeared on his ECAM screen.

"The pilot decided to go back to the gate and report the

problem to the company engineer," the KNKT said in its report. "An engineer came on board and performed trouble shooting on the ECAM. The engineer then reset the Circuit Breakers (see Glossary page 182) of the FAC."

Resetting the FAC when so ordered by the ECAM involved simply pushing a button, but "resetting" the Circuit Breakers (CBs) requires literally removing them and placing them back in. Resetting is a standard action in troubleshooting. Pulling out the CBs is much more radical.

Iriyanto then asked if he could do the same thing if the problem reappeared. The engineer told him he could reset "*whenever so instructed by the ECAM.*"

In other words, the engineer said you must do what the ECAM tells you to do. The engineer didn't endorse the removal and replacement of the CBs, a drastic action that can influence the flight parameters suddenly and cause subsequent degradation of flight control laws.

So the "resetting" of the CBs by the engineer did not have the desired effect, because when the engines were restarted on the second try while the Airbus was on the tarmac before takeoff, the infamous AUTO FLT RUD TRV LIM SYS message reappeared on the ECAM.

The pilot engaged in an intercom conversation with the same engineer who had been on board. The pilot asked the engineer whether he could reset the CBs again and apparently the co-pilot (not Plesel that day) took out the CBs and put them back in again. The problem did not go away, so Iriyanto went back to the parking bay while the passengers were told to wait. Maintenance decided to replace the FAC computer. Apparently, the computer was identified as the source of the problem and AirAsia just happened to have a spare FAC waiting in Surubaya to be installed on another Airbus 320.

"The aircraft flew from Surubaya to Kuala Lumpur and returned without any further problems," states the KNKT report.

It is clear that a maintenance problem on the Airbus 320 was the source of the disaster. There were 23 warnings of defects in the RTLU and still the plane wasn't grounded for an overhaul nor was a thorough examination carried out. Why? The KNKT report suggests a plausible answer to that question: The maintenance staff didn't even consider the possibility that there could be a mechanical issue such as a defective module.

"The workaround solution preferred by the maintenance staff to address the RTLU problems was a computer reset, typically either by resetting the FAC overhead push button followed by an AFS test or by removing the associated CBs. This rectification was performed according to the A320 Trouble Shooting Manual," it reads.

FROM SIMPLE PAIN IN THE NECK TO HELLISH NIGHTMARE

It's not hard to imagine that Captain Iriyanto was terribly annoyed when on that fatal day of Dec. 28, only 30 minutes after take-off, the accursed AUTO FLT RUD TRV LIM SYS message reappeared on the ECAM. We can only guess what went through his mind. "Did the maintenance staff fail to fix the problem?" Or maybe "Do I have to go through the motions again, pushing and resetting the FAC?"

Apparently the captain and his second in command opted for the latter, until the failure became so problematic that the pilots switched to Plan B: To reset the circuit breakers, which caused the two FACS to shut off. There is no proof as to why the FAC's shut down on Flight Q8501, but the KNKT supposes the pilots repeated the same procedure, as three days earlier on the tarmac.

The shutting down of the FAC led to the second phase of the disaster: The disconnection of the Automatic Pilot and Auto Thrust not only handed the control to the pilots, but produced other unexpected and undesired effects. The rudder became positioned with a deflection of 2 degrees. This seems minor, but if sustained it will cause a serious roll. While the pilots were concentrating on taking the controls, the plane made a dramatic roll to the left, reaching a bank angle of no less than 54 degrees. In Normal Law, the bank angle is limited to 33 degrees, but in Alternate Law these protections disappear. It's likely the pilots did not expect such a strong roll. It's noteworthy that a small deflection of only 2 degrees, sustained for only seven seconds, can have such dramatic effects. But they regained control and stabilized the aircraft.

The third phase of the disaster occurred when the pilots started to pitch up, climbing to 38,000 feet. The aircraft then entered into a stall leading quickly to a steep descent. Why would the pilots deliberately pull up and fly into a stall? According to several investigators, including the KNKT's Nurcahyo Utomo, there was a miscommunication between the two pilots. On the cockpit voice recorder one can hear Iriyanto say "pull down, pull down" a couple of times (at 23:17:15 to be exact) and his second in command, Rémi-Emmanuel Plesel, reacted by pulling the stick down (and pitching up), instead of pitching down, which would have been the proper action to take after the first stall alarm had sounded.

The often-criticized double input on the Airbus did the rest. Iriyanto was pitching down, but his inputs were neutralized by Plesel. Would the second in command make this basic, even infantile error or was there a communication problem between two non-native English speakers as has been suggested elsewhere? We will never know.

The three-phase accident – a mechanical fault in the rudder, an unexpected roll to the left, and an incorrect input by a pilot – can be seen as an unfortunate chain of events that led to a fatal crash, but echoes in the international press put the blame right on the pilots: *"AirAsia crash: crew lost control of plane after apparent misunderstanding"* read a headline in The Guardian after the KNKT report was released. A CNN article written by Tiffany Ap was topped with *"Pilot response led to AirAsia crash into Java Sea."* When CNN aviation specialist Richard Quest discussed the AirAsia crash on Dec. 1, 2015, he cited the chain of events, but still pointed at the pilots: "It's a series of technical failures, but it's the pilot response that leads to the plane crashing."

CNN news anchor Rosemary Church then voiced a common misperception about flying on Auto Pilot. She asked Quest "What about the situation where so many pilots now seem to fly putting the planes into Auto Pilot. Is that recommended? Could there be more hands on, so when there is a technical failure they are ready to respond?"

"It's not about Auto Pilot," Quest responded, referencing the difference of flying without Auto Pilot and flying without the protections of Normal Law. "It's about the training of pilots not only in the modern systems of these very sophisticated aircrafts but to handle them when they fail." Quest added, "Only

10 percent of accidents take place in the cruise phase of flight, but if something *does* happen in the cruise phase it tends to be critical and fatal."

A similar view was expressed that same day in The Guardian. The AirAsia crash was compared to the AF447 accident by a leading voice in the business, David Learmount, who also writes for the *FlightGlobal* website. "The incidence of pilots losing control has increased as planes have become more and more automated... Very rarely does anything serious go wrong with the plane or its computers but if it does, the pilots often don't cope."

In line with Quest's comments, Learmount revealed the underlying philosophy that prevails in the airline business: Computers are (almost) perfect. But when they're not, a human being must come to their aid. And fast.

After the KNKT report came out in December 2015, AirAsia owner Tony Fernandes said "there is much to be learned here for AirAsia, the manufacturer and the aviation industry. We will leave no stone unturned to make sure the industry learns from this tragic incident." Fernandes did not issue a mea culpa for the clear maintenance failures that had taken place under his command in AirAsia.

FAMILY MEMBERS TAKE ACTION

Family members of the victims were clearly not satisfied with AirAsia's explanations for the crash. Indonesian businessman Ebenhaezar Tanaputra owns a fashion store and a spare motor parts distribution center in Surubaya. He lost six family members in the crash after he drove them to the airport himself two days after Christmas. "They went on holiday and they never came back," Tanaputra wrote in an email. "Our family still feels sad whenever we think about what happened on December 28, 2014."

Like most victims' families, Tanaputra accepted the compensation offered by AirAsia and its insurer in early 2015. But after the KNKT report highlighted the hidden mechanical and programming failures on the Airbus, the families realized there had been serious negligence. Tanaputra said he immediately felt suspicious about the excuses and explanations offered by AirAsia and he is no longer satisfied with the compensation agreement.

"Our family was forced to agree with the terms of the agreement offered (before we knew the results of the KNKT report)." He wrote that he believes AirAsia lied to the victims' families. Had he known that the crash would be blamed on AirAsia's "carelessness and failure... to fix its plane" he never would have accepted the compensation. The Indonesian businessman does not think the plane crashed because of the pilot, citing the report's conclusion that there was a faulty soldered joint in the rudder system. "All the victims' families now believe it was a faulty plane that led to the accident."

After the KNKT report was published, Tanaputra and other victims' family members contacted the Martin Chico law firm, a French firm specializing in airplane disasters. The firm has handled more than 30 air disaster cases, including the Mont St-Odile crash of an Airbus 320 and the Air France 447 accident. Martin Chico filed a suit against both AirAsia and Airbus and is building a case in a French court. The challenge is not only to prove that AirAsia failed with regard to its maintenance responsibilities, but also that there are fundamental problems with Airbus' fly-by-wire system.

"I don't think we can compare the Air France crash to the AirAsia crash," associate counsel Marc Fribourg told me in a March 2016 interview. "The former happened in very difficult circumstances – at night, during a storm, the pilots did not really recognize what was happening. On the other hand, the AirAsia crash involves a persistent problem that was not handled properly by the maintenance team. It also revealed fundamental problems in the software in Airbus 320 planes."

The lawyers' primary goal is to prove in court that AirAsia and Airbus were guilty of criminal negligence, winning higher damage claims for their clients. "Actually we sue the insurance companies that represent the airline, in this case Artus, which in turn is reinsured by Allianz. Airbus doesn't actually enter the picture at all. Whenever there's a crash, Boeing tends to pay out a part of the settlement. Airbus does not, so in a way that's a way of not admitting guilt."

Fribourg told me that even though accident compensation has been accepted, families still have the right to sue in criminal court, despite AirAsia's insistence that accepting payout means final settlement is agreed on.

To prove AirAsia's liability, the Martin Chico lawyers pored over the case documents and examined all the technical details. In an email exchange that took place in March and April 2016, the founder of the firm, Ricardo Martin Chico, told me that he views the KNKT report skeptically.

"The argument over whether or not the pilots should have reset the FAC, or removed the circuit breakers, is quite sterile," he wrote. "There was a crack in the ACTR 4ACC module, interrupting the connection to the Rudder Traveler Limiter Unit, so restarting the computers had no effect. Instead, the constant restarting of the computers broke the circuitry that was already under stress from extreme weather conditions and variating air pressure."

The defective module was recovered after the crash and a photo in the KNKT report clearly shows where an oxidized piece came loose. It actually looks like a circuit board from a portable radio. "Yes, it's really terrible," Martin Chico told me. "We're talking about a module that might cost... 50 or 100 euros? You wonder why Airbus does not mandate replacing the module every so many flights."

Martin Chico then suggested that the computer-centered troubleshooting of Airbus actually masks real mechanical problems. "The only way to 'fix' it is by resetting the computer. When there is a rudder failure, the only solution proposed is restarting the FAC. But there is no alarm alerting the pilots as to where the problem originated."

Apart from the broken module – a clear failure of in-house maintenance – the Martin Chico lawyers is also focusing on another intriguing A320 flaw: the 2-degree rudder deflection. "On this plane the position of the rudder is permanently recalculated, depending on the inputs and external forces like the wind. It's also calculated with regard to the movements of the ailerons (which control roll and bank). Now... when suddenly no more current reaches the rudder, this one reverts to a previous position by *default*. Therefore, after the automatic pilot disconnected, there was a sudden change in the rudder, which threw the plane off course and caused the roll. In this case, it had fatal consequences. The pilots did not have an option here."

Martin Chico believes the extreme roll to the left (caused by the inappropriate rudder deflection) is an important cause of the crash. Whatever the responsibility of the pilots in the AirAsia crash, the sudden change in rudder position is an Airbus 320 computer design defect, meaning that in certain circumstances this could happen again.

"Actually it already happened before," Fribourg told me in our Skype interview. Fortunately it did not cause the plane to crash so there were no victims. "The A320 rudder glitch as we ought to call it took place on a British Midland flight on Aug. 24, 2010. That day they were flying an Airbus A321 from Khartoum to Beirut when an electrical breakdown occurred. It originated when the electrical breakdown caused an uncommanded application of the rudder trim, causing the aircraft to change direction. The captain was able to manually gain control of the plane and land safely in Beirut. Airbus claimed the electrical power interruption had automatically reset the Flight Augmentation Computer after which the position of the rudder changed spontaneously."

As British Midland was a UK company (the airline has since been acquired by British Airways), the British Air Accidents Investigations Board issued a safety recommendation that year for all airlines that operated the A320 series aircraft. Two important problems with that aircraft were highlighted: 1) an electrical malfunction might not be announced on the ECAM; 2) this electrical malfunction may lead to an uncommanded input of rudder trim.

For the crew and passengers on Flight Q8501, this A320 "problem" wasn't solved on time. The situation was far worse on the AirAsia plane than in the British Midland case, because electrical problems due to faulty circuitry had been known for months, yet maintenance officials failed to make the correct diagnosis. Perhaps more worrisome than the hidden defects on commercial aircraft is the entrenched philosophy that troubleshooting starts with a computer reset, even when the issue is a mechanical failure or a hardware problem.

An Airbus 320 of AirAsia (photo: Pixabay)

CNN report on the *RTLU*-computer glitch after the crash of AirAsia Q 8501.

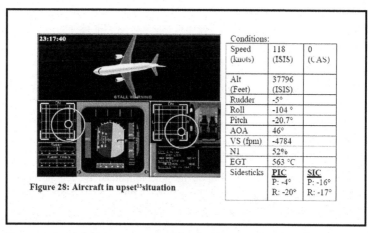

Conditions:				
Speed (knots)	118	(ISIS)	0	(CAS)
Alt (Feet)	37796	(ISIS)		
Rudder	-5°			
Roll	-104 °			
Pitch	-20.7°			
AOA	46°			
VS (fpm)	-4784			
N1	52%			
EGT	563 °C			
Sidesticks	**PIC** P: -4° R: -20°		**SIC** P: -16° R: -17°	

23:17:40

Figure 28: Aircraft in upset[13] situation

Re-enactment of the extreme roll of the Airbus 320 after the automated rudder deflection. (photo: KNKT)

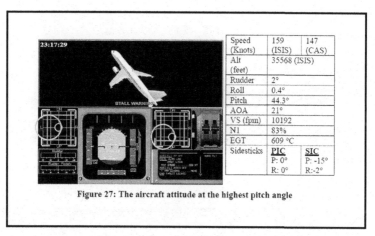

Speed (Knots)	159	(ISIS)	147	(CAS)
Alt (feet)	35568 (ISIS)			
Rudder	2°			
Roll	0.4°			
Pitch	44.3°			
AOA	21°			
VS (fpm)	10192			
N1	83%			
EGT	609 °C			
Sidesticks	**PIC** P: 0° R: 0°		**SIC** P: -15° R:-2°	

23:17:29

Figure 27: The aircraft attitude at the highest pitch angle

Re-enactment of the high pitch angle (more than 40%) when the plane was close to a stall. (photo: KNKT)

Seventeen seconds after the FAC 1 being de-energized, the FDR recorded that the FAC 2 was also de-energized leading to the FAC 1+2 FAULT message. As a consequence the A/P and A/THR disengaged, flight control law reverted from Normal Law to Alternate Law, and the rudder deflected 2° to the left causing the aircraft rolled to the left with rate of 6°/second.

After the auto pilot disengaged the pilot had to fly the aircraft manually. However when the aircraft rolled, neither pilots input the side stick to counter the aircraft roll until nine seconds later thereby the aircraft rolled left up to 54°.

The investigation concluded that the un-commanded roll was caused by the rudder deflection, the autopilot disengaged and no pilot input for nine seconds.

The Indonesian authorities point to the uncommanded rudder movement, after the FAC-computers shut down, causing the roll. (source: KNKT-report)

Close-up of circuit breakers of the A320 Flight Augmentation Computer or FAC.

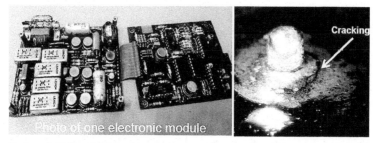

Defect ACTR 4ACC module that caused the malfunction on the Rudder
Travel Limiter Unit on the AirAsia Airbus 320. (photo: KNKT)

Pilot experts and lawyers from the Martin Chico lawfirm in a meeting to define
counter-expertise for the lawsuit against Airbus and AirAsia in French court
(left from right: experts and pilots Jose Maria Oyarzabal and Paco Cruz, lawyer
Marc Fribourg pointing, Ricardo Martin Chico).

CHAPTER 5

–

WHAT DO PILOTS THINK?

In the Argentinean summer of 2016, I was travelling by plane from Buenos Aires to Patagonia. We were greeted by the hostesses and the purser as we stepped onto the plane from the mobile staircase and I asked what model the plane was. The pilot overheard my question, and responded that it was a Boeing 737. A Dutch tourist jokingly interjected: "Airbus is much better!" while giving a thumbs-up, as if to say "European quality rules!"

The pilot smiled courteously and said: "No, I prefer Boeing."

"Oh, really? Why is that?" asked the tourist.

"Boeing is more manual," the pilot said curtly.

The airhostess interrupted the conversation, because we were blocking the doorway. I was surprised by the pilot's comment and felt that I had to speak to him after we reached our destination. Upon landing in El Calafate, I waited until all the other passengers had gone and had a little chat with the pilot. I told him I was interested in his comments. We discussed the Air France case and then he recalled a Lufthansa flight during which "the pilots suddenly lost control."

"That was in November 2014, right? From Bilbao to Frankfurt?"

"Yes, that's the one. It was reported in the press," the pilot said. "A few years ago some colleagues of mine in Aerolineas Argentinas had similar trouble on an Airbus... I think it was somewhere around 2006, if you want I can check it out."

This pilot, Tomas Wechsler, not only confirmed my thesis about pilots not feeling entirely comfortable flying at the mercy of computers, but he was also very open and pleasantly surprised to talk about it with an outsider. Pilots don't talk much about the intricacies of their job with civilians, because they are rarely asked. The general public probably assumes it is too complicated to understand.

It can't be denied that there is an Airbus-Boeing rivalry among pilots. Wechsler was flying in the Boeing division of Aerolineas Argentinas at the time and he clearly preferred the "more manual" Boeing planes, especially the B737. But he had initially flown in the Airbus division of the airline so his was an informed opinion.

Around the same time I met Wechsler, I also got in touch with Airbus pilot Bill Palmer who has become a staunch defender of Airbus planes with solid arguments to back up his position. I also contacted Gérard Arnoux, an Air France captain who is serving as a specialist in the court case on behalf of the AF447 victims' family members.

Finally I spoke with two other Aerolineas Argentinas captains who fly the Airbus 340. I asked for their opinions regarding the AirAsia case and the Air France 447 crash. Much like every pilot I've spoken with, they both made it clear that *an accident is hardly ever the consequence of a single fault or factor. Rather it is usually attributable to a series of errors and failures*, often resulting in a worst-case scenario. Of course, the pilot tends to get the blame because he was the one that was supposed to be in control at the end even if the machine is working against him. Pilot-turned-author Palmer acknowledged this with a hint of irony in the book he published. "He was the one flying the plane after all, wasn't he?" he wrote.

THE AIRASIA CASE

Wechsler had given me his email address and a few weeks later I found myself sitting in a café in Buenos Aires across from my new Aerolineas Argentinas pilot acquaintance. Wechsler had gone over the KNKT report I had sent him by mail and had consented to an interview. "My first impression is that the official report released by the Indonesian Aviation Authority is not complete. Or not very clear at least," Wechsler said, wondering aloud if they had all the information.

He also pointed out that the investigation was carried out by the same airplane constructor that had built the machine. "That's an awkward situation in the aviation world, because the only one who can claim to understand the software on a plane after a crash is the one who built it."

Would you say the crash was the consequence of a pilot error?
Hardly. The machine was already showing the defects on the ground. They should have canceled the flight and done a much more profound maintenance check. Maybe the pilots thought the RTLU fault message was "a spurious fault."

A spurious fault?
Sometimes the computer diagnostic system signals a problem when there is none. Let me give you an example: A colleague of

117

mine was flying an Airbus from Buenos Aires to Auckland (New Zealand) when a message came over the ECAM saying the brakes were overheated. They were in cruise flight so that was very unlikely. Overheating of the brakes might happen after landing or just after taking off: when putting up the landing gear, or when a brake has brushed the wheels… But this was four hours after take-off, so it looked more like a short circuit of the alarm button itself.

These spurious faults are confusing and could have disoriented the AirAsia crew. It's like the boy who cries wolf. After so many incorrect warnings and alerts, the pilots might not have believed it when "the wolf actually came."

Another problem with these fault messages on the ECAM is you don't really know where the problem is located. For instance, you get a message of an *oil bypass* and you know there is a problem with the engine affecting the oil circuit and contaminating it. But as a pilot you don't know exactly what the source of the contamination is. A pilot is not an engineer, so probably he cannot locate the failure in the engine, but nevertheless he's the one in charge of troubleshooting.

Was the RTLU problem critical for the flight?
Maybe the pilots' mistake was that they became *too obsessed* with the RTLU problem, while their priority should have been "Fly the plane!" As a pilot you should always *keep flying the plane*. Even if your engine is on fire, you stabilize the plane first and then you sort out the problems. There is a famous case of a Swissair flight where the pilots were so busy going through the Quick Reference Handbook that they forgot to land. (Wechsler was referring

to Swissair 111, where the captain spent 20 minutes looking through the manual as smoke was coming out of the air conditioning ducts and the cockpit eventually caught fire.) It's all very nice, the lists, and protocol... but the priority was flying.

What exactly is the Quick Reference Handbook?
Part of a pilot's preparation is reading the so-called Quick Reference Handbook (QRH) for troubleshooting. The QRH has lists of things to do in case something goes wrong. On the Boeing 737, we have it in binder form. Airbus has a similar QRH but the book is less-frequently used, because it is accessible via the ECAM screen. (Wechsler rummaged through a briefcase and pulled out a Boeing QRH.) Some of these items are things you need to memorize – you should know what to do without checking the manual. In other cases you must look it up. The co-pilot solves the problem while the pilot keeps on flying.

So you think it was a mistake for the pilots to obsess over resetting?
Sometimes resetting solves the problem, but in this specific case involving the rudder control, it didn't. What is never recommended is pulling out the CBs in flight. This can affect a lot of flight parameters. You could make the situation worse than it already is. Then again, one might ask what would have happened *if they hadn't done anything*. Would the plane have kept flying without any problem? When the computer gives out orders to the controls and they move by themselves – like this 2 percent deflection of the rudder – it can get very dangerous. In the fly-by-wire system, if the computer fails, it can give erroneous orders to the controls.

So this has happened in the past? The computer acted directly on the controls, against the will of the pilots.

Rarely, but it happens. I remember one of my colleagues with Aerolineas Argentinas was flying from New York to Buenos Aires (see page 133). While in cruise flight, all of a sudden the plane pitched up. Reportedly, there was short circuit in a switch on the flight computer. The flight degraded to Alternate Law and the only way they could counter the movement of the elevator was using the trim. They stabilized the plane, reset the computers and finally landed safely in Buenos Aires.

So whenever there's a serious accident, [the authorities and the airlines] never say "they died because there was a short circuit in that electrical part... Or the rudder did whatever it wanted"... They're not going to point out a serious problem with the airplane's computers. The truth is, there are often underlying technical problems and the pilots are in charge of solving these acute problems, of *troubleshooting*.

THE AIR FRANCE CRASH

Troubleshooting was exactly what the pilots on Air France Airbus 330 were busy with on that fateful night in 2009 when their plane went down in the Atlantic. The pilots Bonin and Robert had about 4 minutes after the plane went into Alternate Law and manual mode to keep it flying, but they were unsuccessful. "Actually the day after the accident, I was piloting an Airbus back from Barcelona," Wechsler recalled. "We were on the same route, so when I passed by that area in Northern Brazil of course I thought about what happened the day before."

Did it make you nervous?

No. A pilot always thinks that when there's a problem, he will be able to solve it.

But was the accident on the lips of every pilot?

Yes, the main question was, why did the pilot carry out this strong pitch-up maneuver? But it's easy to play "what if" when you're sitting here with a coffee. They were in a loud cockpit, with alarms going off and contradictory information on their instruments.

Could it be that co-pilot Bonin was misled by the erroneous altitude and vertical speed on the Flight Director?

That's possible. But the fact he was looking at the Primary Flight Display does not mean he shouldn't have stopped looking at his stand-by instruments.

There has been a lot of controversy about the defective pitot tube heating system. But this could hardly be a new problem. What did pilots do before computers were flying the planes?

Sudden loss of reliable airspeed data (Indicated Airspeed, or IAS - see Glossary page 185) is a possibility in flying. The Reference Manuals will tell you exactly what to do at which altitude, when there's a case of unreliable IAS. (Wechsler grabbed his Boeing manual.) Look... here it says: When flying with extended flaps, you should have 10 degrees of pitch and 80% of thrust.

Ten degrees of pitch is a lot.

Yes, but that is flying with the extended flaps, meaning after take-off at low altitudes where one still must gain altitude. One doesn't fly with flaps at great altitudes. You cannot do that at 30,000 feet. At high altitude, according to the manual, one must maintain thrust at 85% of N1 (potential power) and maintain a minimal angle of 2 degrees pitch. Quite a different approach.

Is it possible that Bonin mistook the low-altitude protocol for the high altitude one?
Yes. That's what people in the aviation world say. At those altitudes – we're talking about 30,000 feet – the air gets quite thin and aerodynamically you have to move very smoothly, be careful not to make sudden moves. So the pitch he applied was too much.

So is there a problem with pilot training?
For sure. Most pilots never fly manually; they don't have any experience with this, except in the simulator. They don't even fly manually when they fly without the Auto Pilot! We had a captain in Aerolineas who liked to joke when someone would take off and say "I'm going to be flying manually a while." He'd say, "You are going to fly without the Auto Pilot, but you're not going to fly manually. To do that, I would have to disconnect some computers first." (The captain meant that only then would someone actually be flying without protections.)

So anti-stall training for Airbus pilots was insufficient before the AF447 crash.
Yes. Actually the belief was that an Airbus 330 simply could not stall. That's how Airbus had sold its technology. So there was no need for stall recovery training at high altitudes. After June 1, 2009, Airbus *changed* its stall-recovery protocol, thus admitting

that their old stall-recovery protocol for pilots was inadequate. Before, one had to increase thrust. Nowadays the stall-recovery training focuses on reducing the pitch angle by a few degrees.

The more sophisticated and user-friendly airplanes become in their design, the more a pilot's skills erode. Does a pilot nowadays have enough training to deal with these situations?

In Aerolineas, pilots and co-pilots have to go to the simulator every six months. Other airlines save on that and send their co-pilots only once a year. So, the co-pilot only gets 4 hours of training a year. The computer relieves the workload of the pilots, but that also makes pilots more *entitled*, lazier. For that reason, I personally prefer the more manual Boeing planes. Airbus has some great features, like the Auto Pilot and the APU (Auxiliary Power Unit - see Glossary page 181), which engages automatically. I do find Airbus very comfortable to fly... as long as everything is working well. When something goes wrong, things can get ugly.

BILL PALMER ON THE AIRASIA CRASH

There is a paradox in modern aviation. Let's call it the *concièrge paradox*, to pay tribute to Bernard Ziegler. As modern planes have become more automated, pilots are in danger of losing basic flying skills. As airlines save money on training, they've basically left it up to each pilot to decide how much he wants to keep his skills up-to-date. For instance, pilots can read up on the subject and they can accumulate hours flying smaller manual aircraft.

One pilot who is zealous about studying is Airbus captain Bill Palmer, an American. He wrote "Understanding Air France 447." In an effort to learn more about this accident before writing

the book, he went through the report issued by the BEA as well as the AirAsia 8501 crash report produced by the KNKT. Palmer, apart from flying big passenger jets and smaller aircraft is also an instructor. In addition, he writes articles for a broader public interested in aviation.

With regard to the AirAsia crash, he is quite critical about the actions of the pilots and their responsibility for the crash. However, he recognizes that the problems started with the AirAsia maintenance crew. "AirAsia's maintenance program failed to detect and take action of the repeated trouble with the RTLU," Palmer wrote me in an email in April 2016. "They performed resets in response to Post Flight Reports, contrary to the manufacturer's guidance. This is noted in the (KNKT) report."

The "maintenance program" Palmer refers to are the actions by the engineer who came aboard on Dec. 25 and repeatedly removed and reset the circuit breakers, without making a deeper analysis of the problem. Nevertheless, according to Palmer, the problem with the Rudder Travel Limiter Unit was not of vital importance to the flight. "The rudder itself was working. The mechanical failure (the malfunctioning RTLU) was not critical. They should have left it alone when the ECAM reset didn't completely restore the system. Resetting 3, 4, 5 times is excessive."

The question as to why the rudder deflected, after the shutdown of the computers, is a more complicated matter. According to Palmer, who cites the KNKT report, there was a short delay before the rudder trim electric motor shut down. The total deflection of the rudder was 2 degrees (0.6 degrees original deflection plus 1.4 degrees additional), resulting in an induced roll of 6 degrees per second. This roll, Palmer insists, is significant.

The pilots were not prepared for this.

"The (Pilot Flying) allowed the airplane to roll left to 54 degrees before he took any action and then he had difficulty flying the airplane, made inappropriate control inputs, (and he) failed to recover from a stall that eventually reached Angles of Attack in excess of 45 degrees!"

The pilots created their own problems, Palmer believes, by pulling out the circuit breakers, causing the plane to lose its protections, shifting it to alternate law. "They should have made the reset complete by resetting overhead buttons of the FAC, and then the plane would have gone back to Normal Law."

"They had no business removing the circuit breakers, which was against the reset policy. There was no procedure in the manual that authorized a reset in such a way and they knew it!" Attempting to do maintenance in-flight is a bad idea, Palmer argues, especially when you don't really know what you're doing. There could be unexpected consequences to the intimate details of these systems. "This flight is a perfect example of that."

Independently of the AirAsia case, Palmer has complete confidence in the fly-by-wire concept and automated planes. Does he think humans could eventually be replaced in the cockpit by a computer, as with military drones?

"Military drones still have pilots," Palmer answered in his e-mail. "They're just on the ground in a trailer. Sometimes they lose communication with them. That would not be good on a passenger airplane. An autonomous airliner would have to have a lot more smarts built into it than airplanes do now."

GÉRARD ARNOUX

There are pilots that feel comfortable with automated aircraft and then there are the "old school" pilots who prefer manual flight. Within pilots society there exists some rivalry between those who prefer Airbus and those who prefer Boeing. The American-built planes are considered to be more manual. The Argentinean pilot Tomas Wechsler describes it thusly: "On a Boeing, the computer is there to help the pilot. On an Airbus, the pilot is there to assist the computer."

This difference is quite superficial, since both fully embrace fly-by-wire technology. What both aircraft constructors have in common – and what distinguishes them from car makers – is that they have never been held responsible in the courts for hidden defects in their avionics system.

Gérard Arnoux is not only a former Air France Jumbo captain, he is also a technical advisor in the AF447 case, assisting the victims' families in their suit against Airbus and Air France. He wants to prove Airbus as well as Air France were aware of defects in their machines and did not do enough to prevent an accident and, as such, are guilty of involuntary manslaughter.

Arnoux has read the BEA report diligently, a report he holds in disdain (see Chapter 2). In a Skype conversation, he shared his general thoughts about the role of the pilot.

"A plane must be designed in such a way that the pilots can *understand* what is happening in order for them to take the necessary troubleshooting steps."

In the case of AF477, Arnoux reckoned, Airbus, Air France and the European Air Safety Agency (EASA) shared liability in the build-up to this accident. "It started with the faulty but certified pitot tubes, but there is also an erroneous design of the flying laws," he said. "For the pilots, in the given circumstances, it was almost impossible to regain control over the aircraft."

I asked Arnoux if he thinks pilots are sufficiently trained.

"The current generation of pilots is very intelligent," he said, "but they get little time to practice their manual skills in difficult circumstances. I personally have done quite a few landings in the difficult airport of Calvi (Corsica)." You can see one of the approaches on YouTube.[11]

"It's an approach through the mountains with a sharp turn and tailwind. I've heard that Air France recently published a job posting for 50 pilots to fly regularly to Corsica, but only 20 candidates sent in their resume and this at a time of high unemployment among pilots. The fact is that pilots that fly manually are becoming scarcer."

According to Arnoux, the evolution in civil aviation has reduced job security for pilots. "Since the 80s, aircraft constructors have produced planes that were designed to make pilots superfluous. The original idea was to implement within 20 years a plane without pilot, the so-called *free flight*. We are still in a transitional phase. The general concept seems to be that these civil drones are to be controlled from the ground, by an operator. Of course, this will create other problems, like the threat of hackers."

---

11. "Amazing visual approach in Calvi, Corsica": https://www.youtube.com/watch?v=pHQbBOx5Gz4

ALEJANDRO COVELLO

As I continued with my investigation, I spoke to Alejandro Covello, another Aerolineas Argentinas pilot who has a license to fly the A330 and the A340. (The A340 has four engines whereas the A330 has two engines.). He is still an active pilot and he has flown numerous transatlantic flights. In addition, Covello is a safety specialist with the Investigative Board for Aviation Accidents (JIAAC), the Argentinean counterpart of the NTSB. This makes him a privileged observer in the aviation industry. Covello is not your typical pilot. He holds strong political views. He also makes video documentaries on heroes of the Argentinean Air Force and has written several books.

I interviewed him at his home in a middle-class neighborhood in Buenos Aires. He was between flights and taking a summer writing course.

Automatic systems were created to eliminate pilot error, right?
Yes. In terms of automation on planes, the big change came with the Airbus 320 and the introduction of fly-by-wire. On a modern jet, there are more than 300 computers. Everything is programmed on the ground and then the computers start to work. As a pilot, you are not even aware of what is happening.

Can you give me an example?
Before automation, in order to start the engines we had to keep our hand on the throttle. When the fuel temperature rose, we had to cut the fuel supply because you could lose the engines. On an Airbus nowadays, you flip the fuel switch up and, after that, it's hands off. When it gets too hot, a

computer called the Fadec will bleed fuel to prevent the temperature from rising too much. It will also stop the ignition. It's marvelous, really. But there is an opacity between the operator and, for instance, some valve that moves somewhere in the engine. You really are not aware of what is happening.

And is that good or bad?
It's perfect. Statistics show that accidents have decreased. But here's what happens: The introduction of new technology solves old problems, but at the same time this new technology introduces new problems.

For instance?
I am thinking of the Boeing 757 that crashed near Cali in 1995. (American Airlines Flight 965 crashed in Colombia on Dec. 20, 1995, killing 159 people.) The pilots entered a waypoint in the navigation system but the computer had two different waypoints with the same name (Rozo NDB) and sent the plane in the wrong direction. The plane flew north toward Bogota – instead of south toward Cali – and crashed into a mountain near Buga. Before, you had manual navigation but now the computer does the job, and this can be tricky.

So the pilots got confused about what the machine was doing.
When you hear cockpit recordings, you often hear: "What is happening?... Where is the plane going?" In the Cali crash for instance, the pilots did not take command of the plane. When they finally took over, they already were at risk. When the plane is doing something you don't want it to, you must make

a decision: I am going to disconnect, the plane is mine and I will go back to basics. Many pilots though rely too much on the computer. They give it another opportunity.

Like with your Aerolineas Argentinas colleague who was flying from New York in 2004 and suffered a sudden pitch-up.
They did what they had to do, disconnect the computer and fly manually. The problem is that, with automation, instruction for pilots has changed. We are monitors instead of pilots. You lose flight sensation. Flying with a joystick is the same sensation as being behind the computer with a joystick. You *imagine* the sensation.

Since recent high-profile accidents like Air France, have new instructions come out? Like flying more manually?
Yes, this is happening. Disconnect the computer and fly manually. In the simulator at least. It's interesting to consider, for instance, how long we fly manually on an international flight.

Twenty minutes?
No. Just 5 minutes, 8 minutes... over the course of 12 hours! We are talking about take-off and then after 30 seconds, at 100 feet, you can already switch on the Auto Pilot. And then, each pilot can decide when to disconnect the AP, at 1,000 feet, 300 feet, or at... 200 feet. We are not flying at all.

The A340 can fly by itself?
No, you still need to take off manually; you have to take the plane up to 50 feet...

You never experienced a problem?

Never. The plane is very sure, does everything right, everything one can imagine. When you hear of accidents, these are cases where the plane does strange things and that's when the plane needs to hand over command to me. I am there for what the computer cannot do. The plane will do whatever the engineers thought was possible. The pilot must take over during situations and scenarios the engineers didn't foresee. When the Airbus 320 was launched, they joked that it could be flown by a monkey. One of Airbus' ideas was to remove the co-pilot from the cabin. And then paradoxically, there was the accident when the A320 was exhibited in France...

Habsheim?

Exactly. That put an end to the idea of removing the co-pilot (leaving only one pilot in the cockpit).

What do you think of the way the AF447 pilots reacted?

There are situations that we as pilots practice in a simulator: engine failure, depressurization. A pilot is anticipating that these things might happen, because he has trained for that. This is not what happened to the pilots of Air France. Their pitot tubes got clogged, they lost speed information, they went into alternate law, and then the plane kept trying to correct things based on the wrong information. I can assure you, if you put 100 pilots in that situation, 90 pilots will react the same way. It's an unexpected scenario.

The newspapers reported the pilots went out on the town in Rio the night before, and then on the flight the younger pilot was flying and the captain went to the bunk, leaving the plane in the hands of the less experienced one.

After that accident, Airbus changed the procedures for how to recover from a stall, essentially admitting that their anti-stall training was wrong. Before, you had to increase thrust and lower the nose. That was for stalls at low altitudes – we didn't train for stalls at 30,000 feet, with a heavy plane. You shouldn't forget that way up there, you are much closer to the margins, especially when you are at or near maximum weight. (The AF447 had taken off recently and was loaded with fuel). If you are flying lower, you can move between 160 and 360 knots. In thin air, you might have only 40 knots of leeway between high speed and low-speed stall. I repeat: you put 10 crews in there and with nine crews, the same thing happens. I doubt strongly that they could have recovered from the stall with the old Airbus methods.

Have you ever gone into Alternate Law?
Yeah, I think so.

Is that a reason to panic?
No.

How do you know you are in Alternate Law?
The ECAM warns you. It recommends you to fly lower, around 4,000 feet. So that provides more margin of speed.

Did you know at the time why you went into Alternate Law?

No, you're only informed why it happened after you land, like maybe one of the defense systems, or protections, failed. On the Airbus, there are 5 protections. You lose one and you go into Alternate Law. Another fails, and then you go into Direct Law (manual).

So would you say the system on a Boeing is less complicated and more transparent?

I wouldn't think so. Automation has also taken place with Boeing; there have been high-profile accidents, like the one in the Dominican Republic in 1996 (see Chapter 6, Birgenair Flight). The cause of that accident actually was quite similar to what happened with Air France in 2009.

A SHORTCUT IN A COMPUTER SWITCH

In April 2017, I had the opportunity to chat with the Aerolineas Captain who experienced the aircraft upset in December 2004, the incident mentioned at the beginning of this chapter. The Aerolineas Argentinas pilot (who wants to remain anonymous) was flying an Airbus 340 from New York to Buenos Aires when he experienced an unexpected pitch-up.

What happened?

We were cruising on Auto Pilot, when suddenly the plane pitched up. There are 5 flight computers (on an Airbus 340), the primary or PRIM 1, 2, 3, and the secondary or SEC 1 and SEC 2. There was a shortcircuit in a switch on one PRIM, and that computer assumed it was failing, so it shut itself down.

After this, the other computers also shut themselves down. We were suddenly flying *mechanically* (manually), so we used the trim to counter the elevator.

Were you scared?
We didn't have time to be scared. There were three of us in the cockpit and we worked well together. We didn't understand what was happening at the time. Actually there were some cargo pallets loaded in New York and we thought the cargo had shifted and this had made the plane pitch up. After 40 minutes the situation was completely normal again. After we landed in Ezeiza International Airport in Buenos Aires, the computers were sent to Toulouse where they discovered the computer wasn't at fault... it was just a switch.

As a result of this investigation, Airbus issued an internal directive ordering the switches on the computers to be changed after a certain amount of time, even if they were fairly new, as was true in our case. Another result of this upset was that Airbus changed the software on the computers. It wasn't normal for one faulty computer to contaminate the others and make the others shut down.

The idea is that the computers are supposed to be redundant...
Yes. The back-up computers apparently took information from the first computer. A few weeks later, a committee from Airbus came to Buenos Aires to talk to the pilots about the upset and what should be done when this happens. I wasn't there because I was flying at that time, but I heard of the meeting. Something else I've noticed is that after our experience, the

item in our Quick Reference Handbook regarding a pitch-up in cruise flight was taken out...

Have you had any other experience like that?
No, never. For me the Airbus 340 is a wonderful plane. It's very well designed. It has some revolutionary features like fuel storage in the trim tail. The fuel is pumped there to shift the center of gravity, depending on the phase of flight. I really like flying it (the A340). Before Airbus, you had to move the fuel levers to control the fuel. Now, it is all done automatically.

Do you think there is a risk that pilots get too relaxed and lose their reflexes because of automation?
There is a difference between pilots that fly long-haul, trans-oceanic flights like me and pilots that fly domestic flights. On international flights, you are always with other pilots in the cockpit so you don't do all the take-offs and landings. So how many take-offs and landings do you do each month? Two or three. This might erode your flying skills a bit so you'll need extra training on a simulator. A pilot who does domestic flights might do four or five landings a day and so has much more practice this way.

Cockpit of an original Boeing 737 from the eighties: a collection of instruments, dials, switches and gauges. (photo: Venancio Ozino)

A "glass" Cockpit of an A340 in service: the amount of instruments is reduced dramatically and integrated in LCD-computer screens. (photo: Venancio Ozino)

136

Aerolineas Argentinas pilot Tomas Wechsler, currently flying Boeing 737.

American pilot and instructor Bill Palmer in a glider.

Aerolineas Argentinas A340, four-engine version of the A330, landing at Fiumicino Airport (Rome), flying in from Buenos Aires. Both Captain Covello and Captain Fiallegas fly this plane.

Alejandro Covello, Aerolineas Argentinas pilot (Airbus 340) and video director.

CHAPTER 6

–

DIFFERENT COMPANIES, SIMILAR PROBLEMS

Although Airbus is considered the reference for fly-by-wire and automation, its big U.S. competitor Boeing has taken the same direction. Since the 1990s, Boeing development also focused on avionics and fly-by-wire. Since then, the U.S. aircraft manufacturer has also suffered several fatal accidents due to flaws traced to on-board computers.

One example of the new modern planes built by the Seattle-based giant is the Boeing 757, from the same generation as the Airbus 320. This midsize twin engine was launched commercially in 1983 and it was Boeing's largest single-aisle airplane at that time. (The last B-757 was produced in 2004).

The Boeing 757 could seat up to 295 passengers for short and medium routes and just like its sister plane – the B-767 – the aircraft featured a basic form of fly-by-wire (to operate the spoilers) and the so-called "glass cockpit," wherein the traditional analog dials and gauges in the cockpit were replaced by digital flight instrument displays on an LCD screen.

Another novelty on the B-757 and B-767 was the Flight Management Computer (FMC - see Glossary page 183). The

FMC carries out many in-flight tasks, such as programming the flight plan, the navigator's or on-board engineer's most time-consuming job. With the adoption of the FMC and the incorporation of avionics on the B-757, the flight engineer became superfluous. The number of crew members in the cockpit was reduced from three to two, the pilot and the co-pilot. This is exactly what happened on the Airbus 320.

The B-757 proved to be a big success. Although it had a limited range and was not built for long transatlantic flights, it became a standard plane for medium-range flights connecting US cities. Once it was formally certified, it also made regular flights between Europe and New York. It boasted an excellent safety record until 1995, when, in the course of 10 months, three B-757s crashed: one in Colombia, one in the Dominican Republic and another in Peru. The latter two accidents bear striking similarities to the Air France 447 crash, not the least with regard to the confusion in the cockpit and problems with the instruments.

BIRGENAIR FLIGHT 301

German-Turkish charter airline Birgenair Flight 301 was full of German nationals on Feb. 6, 1996, as it took off from Puerto Plata in the Dominican Republic, heading to Frankfurt, Germany. Most of the passengers were tourists who had been on a beach holiday. Not long after take-off, as the aircraft was climbing at 4,700 feet, the Auto Pilot made the plane pitch up and reduced power. The captain's Airspeed Indicator (ASI - see Glossary page 179) was showing a speed of 350 knots (650 km/h), considered too fast for that particular phase of flight. Since the Auto Pilot was getting its information from the same source, it decided to pitch up and reduce throttle in order to slow down. After this pitch-up maneuver, the Auto Pilot disconnected. In the cockpit, the pilots were receiving contradictory information: The overspeed alarm went off and the overspeed light flashed on, indicating both rudder ratio and Mach airspeed had been surpassed. So the pilots reduced thrust more. But on the co-pilot's instruments, the ASI speed had fallen to 200 knots, suggesting that the aircraft was flying too slowly. This seemed to be the situation because the stick-shaker stall alert was triggered. (On a Boeing, the yoke starts to shake before a stall.) The aircraft was actually flying too slowly with an excessive Angle of Attack.

The captain immediately understood that the aircraft was in danger of stalling and he increased thrust to full throttle. However, the Angle of Attack was too high due to the earlier inputs (of the now disengaged Auto Pilot) and there was not enough airflow coming into the engines. This caused one of the engines to shut down, throwing the aircraft into a spin from which it did not recover. The Boeing 757 crashed into the ocean and all 189 people on board were killed. It is the biggest disaster to date for a Boeing 757.

Although the initial problem was clearly caused by the Auto Pilot, the machine itself was exonerated and the culprits were identified elsewhere. The Dominican Republic's Aeronautical Investigation Board (DGAC) concluded that the cause of the crash was "the crew's failure to recognize the activation of the stick shaker as a warning of imminent entrance into a stall, and the failure of the crew to execute the procedures for recovery from the onset of loss of control." In other words, the pilots failed to recover control of the plane.

The same report also pointed a finger at another possible culprit, a very unlikely one: the black and yellow mud dauber, or "cement wasp." This insect, which is quite common in the Dominican Republic, tends to builds its nest with mud and one or more nests could have clogged the pitot tubes.

This was merely an assumption since the pitot tubes were never recovered. The DGAC speculated "that the plane had been on the ground for 20 days and wasps could have made a nest, since the pitot tubes could have been uncovered and not protected by tape." Birgenair contested that information and said the pitot tubes were covered during most of the plane's stay-over.

Still, the possible presence of such a nest seems like a speculative argument designed to deflect questions about the faulty Auto Pilot, and the misguided tasks it carried out due to false speed readings which effectively put the plane in a stall situation. We can't dismiss the supposition that the captain might have followed the incorrect airspeed indications even if he had been flying manually. This too would have slowed down the plane and resulted in a pitch-up, but his co-pilot might have pointed out the correct readings on his airspeed indicator.

In any case, as often happens, the pilots were not given the benefit of the doubt, and they now carry the responsibility for the crash. Birgenair went bankrupt after the crash demonstrating that it is much harder for a small airline to survive a deadly accident than a big one such as Air France.

AEROPERU FLIGHT 603

Eight months after the Birgenair 301 crash, another Boeing 757 went down, this time because the Flight Management Computer (FMC) went haywire.

On Oct. 2, 1996, a Boeing 757 operated by AeroPeru had just taken off from Lima when the pilots were confused by erratic flight instruments and problems with the FMC. Just like on the Birgenair flight, the FMC was reporting contradictory emergency messages: Alarms indicated problems with the rudder ratio, Mach speed trim, overspeed as well as underspeed while also indicating that the plane was flying too low.

The pilots decided to return to the airport and began to descend, but because of unreliable instruments, they were flying lower than they believed. A wingtip hit the water and the plane crashed into the ocean.

The investigation into the AeroPeru Flight 603 crash did not find blame with wasps this time, instead pointing the finger at a maintenance operator. The report declared that the maintenance man had covered the static ports with duct tape while cleaning the fuselage and had forgotten to take the tape off after finishing. These static ports are fundamental for recording basic flight information including speed and altitude. Of course, it's always easier to blame the low man on the totem pole (the maintenance man in question, Eleuterio Chacaliaza, was convicted of involuntary homicide and was sentenced to two years in prison). In this manner, the investigators chose not to question a computer system that, instead of shutting off when a blockage exists, displays erroneous and deceptive information in the cockpit.

Although the earlier Boeing 757 and 767 models featured some fly-by-wire controls, the first fully fly-by-wire aircraft from Boeing was the 777, also known as the "triple 7." It was introduced commercially in 1995 and is still being produced today. The 777, a wide body aircraft made for long-haul routes, has been very successful commercially due to its fuel efficiency. It is considered the natural competitor to the Airbus twin engine A330.

The Boeing 777 model became infamous in 2014. That's when Malaysian Airlines Flight 17 was shot down over Donetsk by pro-Russian militia and Malaysian Airlines Flight 370 disappeared mysteriously over the Indian Ocean, probably because of a dramatic depressurization.

But there was an earlier incident involving a Malaysian Airlines B-777. On Aug. 1, 2005, Malaysian Airlines Flight 124 took off from Perth on its way to Kuala Lumpur in Malaysia.[12] According to the Australian Transport Safety Bureau (ATSB) investigation, the pilots suddenly saw contradictory information on both Primary Flight Displays: A message said the plane was approaching both the high-speed limit and the low-speed limit. At that time the Auto Pilot was engaged.

As the plane climbed through 38,000 feet, it suddenly pitched up and climbed to 41,000 feet. Due to the sudden climb, the airspeed decreased from 270 knots to 158 knots, bringing the machine close to a stall causing the stall alarms to go off. The Pilot Flying disconnected the Auto Pilot and

---

12. The full report: http://www.atsb.gov.au/publications/investigation_reports/2005/AAIR/pdf/aair200503722_001.pdf

lowered the nose of the aircraft. The Autothrottle then commanded an increase in thrust that the Pilot Flying countered by manually moving the thrust levers to the idle position. After this, the aircraft pitched up again and climbed another 2,000 feet.

The pilots were able to regain control over the aircraft and they decided to return to Perth. During the return, the crew activated Auto Pilot again and the aircraft began to pitch down, while banking to the right.

Because of this, the pilots shut down Auto Pilot for the second time and began to fly the plane manually. "The pilot in command reported that, with the Auto Pilot disengaged, there were no further control difficulties experienced," the ATSB report reads. However, when the plane reached 3,000 feet, another erroneous low airspeed warning appeared on the Flight Display. The Autothrottle responded by pushing forward the thrust levers to increase speed and to avoid a stall that was not actually in danger of occurring. Since the pilot was able to override the Autothrottle command simply by manually adjusting the thrust levers, the pilots were able to land safely at Perth. Luckily, there were no injuries on this unsettling flight. Boeing proponents argue that it has an advantage over Airbus because it has "real throttles" that the pilot can use to override an engaged Autothrottle.

It's clear that the pilots did an excellent job, not only counteracting the Auto Pilot and Autothrottle, but also flying the plane manually despite false speed indications on the screen.

The ATSB came to a startling conclusion. The Auto Pilot had not behaved erratically due to malfunctioning external sensors (as on the Birgenair and AeroPeru flights). Instead, the ATSB found evidence of software errors within the flight computer itself!

According to the ATSB, the incident was caused by a software error in the Air Data Inertial Reference Unit, or ADIRU (see Glossary page 178). These ADIRUs are the computers that collect all these data such as airspeed, Angle of Attack and altitude and transmit this to the flight systems.

The ADIRU gets its information from pitot tubes and static ports and the Auto Pilot and the flight instruments depend on this information. After the incident on Flight 124, it became clear that the onboard computers are not always faultless.

The ATSB investigation found that there was a software error in the ADIRU, allowing it to use data from a defective accelerometer. The accelerometer – not the same as a speedometer or a pitot tube – is an electromechanical device that measures acceleration forces and is an essential part of the ADIRU.

After this worrisome incident, the U.S. Federal Aviation Administration (FAA) issued an Emergency Airspeed Indicator (see Glossary page 179) requiring all B-777 operators to install upgraded software to resolve the error on the ADIRU. Due to the importance of this external data, there is always a redundant back-up unit provided for the ADIRU, the SAARU. But on Malaysian Flight 124, this back-up information wasn't displayed. There was likely a failure of the back-up system too.[13]

ADIRU FAILURES ON AN AIRBUS

There seems to be a jinx on the Malaysian Airlines Boeing 777 aircrafts involved in the previously mentioned incident and the

---

13. Robert J. Boser, Editor in Chef of Airline Safety, reported on the Flight 124 investigation: http://www.airlinesafety.com/faq/777Data-Failure.htm

disasters with Flight 17 and Flight 370. Oddly enough, there also seems to be a curse on flights near Perth and Australia's west coast. An incident similar to what happened aboard Flight 124 occurred three years later in that very region, this time involving an Airbus 330, the main competitor for the Boeing 777.

This case involved the same Airbus 330 model as the fatal Air France Flight 447 crash that would occur a year later.

On Oct. 7, 2008, Qantas Flight 72 was flying from Singapore to Perth. It was cruising at 37,000 feet when the Auto Pilot disengaged. The aircraft then suffered two sudden uncommanded pitch-down maneuvers, causing the plane to plunge in a 650-foot nosedive. The incident caused injuries to 74 passengers and crew, from broken bones to spinal injuries. Fortunately, the pilots were able to make an emergency landing, avoiding further casualties.

As a result of the serious injuries, the incident was widely reported in the Australian media and the ATSB opened an investigation. The aircraft's ADIRUs were sent to the manufacturer Northrop Grumman for testing.

The ATSB later reported that there had been a failure within one ADIRU. "These very high, random and incorrect values of the Angle of Attack led the Flight Control computers to order a nose-down aircraft movement, which resulted in the aircraft pitching down to a maximum of about 8.5 degrees," it stated according to an ABC News Australia report from Oct. 14, 2008. "Even with the Auto Pilot off, the plane's Flight Control computers still command key controls in order to protect the jet from dangerous conditions, such as stalling."

149

The ATSB report simply confirms the way the Airbus safety envelope works: Though the Auto Pilot was disconnected, judging the external air reference data to be incorrect, the ADIRU-generated data still influenced the plane's protection envelope, as Qantas Flight 72 was flying in Normal Law. Paradoxically, by assuming the plane was entering a stall, the safety envelope actually put the lives of the passengers in danger.

That same aircraft had experienced problems with its ADIRU two years earlier, flying from Hong Kong to (again) Perth. On Sept. 12, 2006, Qantas Flight 68 was flying over Western Australia when errors in the ADIRU were reported as problems on the ECAM. After several warnings and caution messages, the crew decided to turn off the ADIRU-1 and the pilots kept flying without any adverse effect on the flight controls. After this event, the manufacturer (Northrop Grumman) recommended maintenance procedures and system testing, but no defects were found. However, the same ADIRU failed two years later on the above-mentioned Flight 72, nearly resulting in tragedy.

THE FAA TAKES ACTION

These failures are still occurring and therefore the authorities, like the US Federal Aviation Administration (FAA), issue Airworthiness Directives or ADs (See glossary) to limit possible ADIRU breakdowns.

In November 2013, for instance, the FAA issued a new AD for the Airbus A330-series, superseding earlier Airworthiness Directives[14]. The earlier ADs had required the inclusion in the

---

14. AD2011-02-09 and AD2009-04-07 were replaced by AD2013-19-14

A330 flying manual of a procedure to prevent the ADIRU from feeding erroneous data to other airplane systems.

The 2013 AD, on the other hand, required operators to modify or replace all three flight control primary computers with *new software standards*. "We are issuing this AD *to prevent autopilot engagement under unreliable airspeed conditions, which could result in reduced controllability of the airplane,*" the AD read[15]. Apparently, the FAA had come to the conclusion that the software on the ADIRUs was not working well and that operational procedures by pilots, were not sufficient to solve these problems. A software update was imperative.

The FAA also issued warnings about the ADIRUs on the Airbus 320 models.

In a Jan. 27, 2004, Airworthiness Directive, the FAA called for "modification to the mounting of ADIRU-3 in Airbus A320 aircraft." Four years later, an August 2008 airworthiness directive superseded the older directive by requiring the immediate replacement of faulty ADIRUs on the Airbus 320 to prevent failure of an ADIRU in-flight, *which could result in the loss of one source of critical attitude and airspeed data, reducing the ability of the flight crew to control the airplane.*

In other words, the FAA had first suggested mounting the malfunctioning ADIRUs in a different order on the shelf in the avionics compartment before deciding upon the outright replacement of those units.

---

15. https://www.federalregister.gov/documents/2013/11/14/2013-26565/airworthiness-directives-airbus-airplanes

Even the most respectable airlines and those with spotless safety records are not beyond risks. A good example is the Nov. 5, 2014, Lufthansa flight from Bilbao to Munich. An Airbus 320 was climbing at 31,000 feet when the plane pitched down abruptly and dived with a vertical speed of 4,000 feet per minute. The flight crew was able to counteract the computer's orders and stabilized the plane at 27,000 feet. The plane landed safely in Munich, but not until after the passengers got the scare of their lives.

The German aircraft accidents investigators, the BFU, conducted an investigation and found out that the onboard computers had sent the plane into the dive because the Angle of Attack sensors had frozen. These sensors are vane-like devices on the side of the plane that move according to incoming airflow. With the sensors inoperable, the on-board computers assumed the plane had entered a stall during the climb and automatically ordered a pitch-down.

The crew could not counteract these fly-by-wire commands, although they applied full back stick input. The plane was still within the protections of Normal Law and the pilot's actions were limited. The only solution was to shut down the ADIRU, which was responding to the erroneous external data.[16]

After this event in 2014, the European Aviation Safety Agency (EASA) issued an emergency airworthiness directive on how pilots can counteract these events and how the Airbus Quick Reference Handbook should be amended to include these situations. "The EASA directs that only one Air Data

16. For more information on this Lufthansa incident, see:
http://avherald.com/h?article=47d74074

Inertial Reference Unit (ADIRU) be kept operative while turning off the other two in the following cases: *1. The aircraft goes into a continuous nose-down pitch movement that cannot be stopped by full backward stick deflection. 2. The Alpha Max (red) strip completely hides the Alpha Prot strip (black/amber) without increase in load factor. 3. The Alpha Prot strip rapidly changes by more than 30 knots during flight maneuvers with increase in load factor while Auto Pilot is on and speed brakes are retracted."*

This directive reveals that the EASA believes that in an emergency situation, when every second counts, the pilots have the time to go through their Quick Reference Handbook to decide what course of action to take. These procedures have nothing to do with flying skills, but with the management of onboard computers and software.

MCDONNELL DOUGLAS: SPANAIR FLIGHT JK5022

The financial pressures of commercial aviation often lead to attempts to cover up hidden technical defects on planes, like defects unintentionally built into the design that only show up under extraordinary circumstances.

Other hidden defects can be components that have become worn out or pass their expiration date without being recognized and dutifully replaced by maintenance crews. A good example is the AirAsia flight and the component that affected the RTLU. The reality is that once an aircraft has left the manufacturers' hangar maintenance is in the hands of the airline. In every country, local transportation officials are responsible for certifying the airworthiness of aircrafts, but too often these offices are understaffed.

On Aug. 20, 2008, there were only two air inspectors on the job in all of Spain. So there was virtually no chance one of these two would have grounded Spanair's McDonnell Douglas 82 (McDonnell Douglas merged with Boeing in 1996) before it departed from the Madrid airport. However, there were very good reasons for Flight JK5022 to be canceled on that hot summer day. After pulling away from the gate, the pilots noticed an abnormal rise in temperature on an external temperature probe called the RAT (Ram Air Temperature probe) and the external temperature is a necessary element to calculate True Airspeed.

Since that very same probe had overheated the day before, the pilots decided to go back to the gate. A mechanic entered the cockpit and started discussing what might be causing the overheating. Citing the outside temperature (it was summer in Madrid), the possibility of cooling down the probe with dry ice was mentioned, a temporary solution that had seemed to work on previous occasions.

The mechanic thought there might be something wrong with the de-icing system of the probe (like the pitot tubes on AF447) and that the de-icing system was on while the aircraft was on the ground. Since the aircraft would not be encountering icing conditions from Madrid to the Canary Islands, he decided to shut off the power for the de-icing mechanism.

The plane rolled to the head of the runway and the pilots went through the checklist. According to the Cockpit Voice Recorder, they apparently skipped the "check flaps and slats" item. Before take-off, the flaps and slats must be deployed (to give the plane the necessary lift) but the Spainair pilots were taking off with their flaps retracted. To prevent this, aircrafts like the McDonnell Douglas-82 have an automatic alarm – the Take Off Warning System, or TOWS – to warn the pilots the plane is not properly configured for take-off. The TOWS alarm did not work that day.

The MD-82 went down the runway and took off but did not gain altitude, crashing soon thereafter with a toll of 154 dead, the third-deadliest accident in Spain's history.

The Spanish Civil Aviation Accident and Incident Investigation Commission (CIAIAC, its acronym in Spanish) conducted an investigation, issuing its report in 2011. The pilots were blamed for not checking the slats-flaps items. The temperature-probe issue gets a mention, but only as part of the timeline of events preceding take-off and not as a possible cause of the crash.

As in other air disasters, the victims' family members organized to obtain more information. They were infuriated that the CIAIAC report did not thoroughly examine the MD-82's electronic problems. "These are 308 pages to conceal the truth," victims' organizations president Pilar Vera said.

"Everything about the official report is outrageous," said Juan Carlos Lozano, a member of the international pilot union's investigation committee. "There are powerful interests and powerful people who have been left off the hook. They have not been very brave in this investigation."

Lozano pointed out that there had been similar problems with non-functioning flaps on other aircraft in the MD-80 series. Only a year before, in June 2007, on Lanzarote (an island near the Gran Canaria), another MD operated by the Spanish airline Air Comet almost crashed because it took off without its flaps deployed. The pilots had succeeded in keeping the plane in the air after some acrobatic movements including a 55-degree banked turn that saw the plane scrape over a car dealership. Bystanders threw themselves to the ground.

American pilot James Hudspeth, an MD pilot for Austrian company Mapjet with more than 17,000 flight hours, had flown to Lanzarote to investigate the event and what he found was quite startling. The day before the near-fatal incident, the external temperature probe was very hot. The mechanics concluded that a circuit breaker had tripped and they repaired it. The next day, the Air Comet MD-83 took off without its flaps deployed and the TOWS alarm did not go off. Hudspeth found that both the RAT probe and the TOWS alarm depended on the same relay or circuit breaker (Relay R2-5 from the Leach Corporation). The circuit breaker is active or inactive, depending on whether a plane is on the ground or in flight mode. This makes sense, because flaps are usually retracted in flight and the probe heating or de-icing system becomes active. Hudspeth also found that maintenance crews often removed these relays to test the flight configuration, and occasionally would forget to put them back in.

Although a pilot should ultimately check his plane to make sure all the circuit breakers are in place, they are not visually clear when the white-colored ring gets dirty, making it easy to overlook. Hudspeth reported that at his own airline – Mapjet, which had three MDs – the relays had not been plugged in on at least six occasions. Hudspeth suggested that the Spanair accident could have been caused by inactive (or broken) Circuit Breakers, leading to the wrong flight configuration.

"The incident with the Air Comet in Lanzarote did not lead to a tragedy, because the MD-83 has more powerful engines and there was strong headwind to help it gain altitude," Hudspeth explained in an interview he did with Spanish newspaper El País on Oct. 5, 2008.

Hudspeth took his conclusions to the CIAIAC in early 2008, arguing that the circuit breakers on the MD-80 series could lead to confusion about flight configuration. The CIAIAC declined to take any action and did not include the Lanzarote incident in its 2011 report on the Spanair crash.

After the Spanair crash, Hudspeth was disturbed because of the striking similarities of what had happened a year earlier in Lanzarote. Hudspeth later talked to the press, admitting he was upset his investigation had not helped to prevent the crash. "I feel guilty, but I warned the Spanish investigative commission (CIAIAC) last January that an accident like that could occur and they didn't do anything," he said. "I just don't want it happen to again." The same person that interviewed Hudspeth in 2008 was the chief CIAIAC investigator in the Spanair case, according to Juan Carlos Lozano.

Another detail is that most systems on the MD-82 are informed about the ground or flight configuration through redundant relay circuit breakers: So called left and right control relays. Hudspeth discovered that the TOWS and the RAT probe depend exclusively on the left relay circuit breaker. If this circuit breaker were removed or broken, the TOWS alarm would be inactive without the pilot's knowledge. If the Spanish commission had done its job and taken Hudspeth's investigation seriously, they could have identified this lack of redundancy and the potential risk on the MD-80 series airplanes. The fact that the RAT probe overheated would have been a clear signal the TOWS was not working.[17]

The similarities with the 2014 AirAsia crash are striking. It is basically unforgivable that an electrical failure that could have been prevented by the timely replacement of a basic component like a circuit breaker cost 154 human lives. "This item might cost something like ... 50 euros," says Rafael Vidal, one of the few survivors of the crash. This is eerily reminiscent of what attorney Ricardo Martin Chico said about the defective module that controlled the RTLU. "Everybody agrees," Vidal, an electronic engineer says, "that if the TOWS alarm would have worked – which is not only a visual alarm but also a distinctively loud noise – the crew would never have taken off. But the CIAIAC report does not include one word about *why* the alarm failed. They just say it didn't work. Period. And that it had nothing to do with the RAT heating system. That's a joke and an insult to the victims."

DASSAULT FALCON IN MALAYSIA (2011)

The more sophisticated aircraft become and the more they are crammed with electronics, the more likely it is that a tiny glitch or a minor failure can have fatal consequences. A circuit breaker on Spanair 5022, a pitot probe heater failure on AF447, an electronic module on AirAsia 8501 all led to disasters.

Although commercial aviation has become very safe over the last several decades, system failures continue to be an underrated

---

17. Spanair victims' family members made a video detailing the crash investigation's errors, Una Cadena de Errores (A Chain of Errors): http://jk5022achainoferrors.com

problem. Even Harro Ranter, the founder of Aviation Safety Network, a non-profit organization that catalogues all accidents and incidents with aircrafts, knows this. Asked about this phcnomenon, he sent me an email about an incident in 2011 involving a business jet.

"On May 25, 2011, a Dassault Falcon 7X departed Nuremberg, Germany, on a flight to Kuala Lumpur in Malaysia with two crew members on board. While descending through 13,000 feet toward Kuala Lumpur, the elevator pitch trim began to move from neutral to the full nose-up position within a 15-second timeframe. This resulted in a sudden pitch-up of the aircraft to 40 degrees and the aircraft entered a climb. Initially both the captain (Pilot Monitoring) and the copilot (Pilot Flying) were using the side stick in an attempt to regain control... The co-pilot, a former military pilot with experience on Mirage jets, put the aircraft into a right-hand bank to a maximum of 98 degrees.

Eventually the pitch attitude decreased. After 2 minutes and 35 seconds, the crew was able to regain control of the airplane again. Meanwhile, the aircraft had reached an altitude of 22,500 feet.[18] The passengers in the Dassault plane experienced a real rollercoaster ride, like they'd been on a fighter jet, with a bank angle of 98 degrees! After this incident, the BEA did an investigation and grounded the Dassault jets for three weeks. In its report, the BEA concluded that 'there was a factory defect in the Horizontal Stabilizer Electronic Control Unit (HSECU) due to defective soldering of a pin of this chip.'[19]

---

18. https://news.aviation-safety.net/2016/02/15/ serious-incident-report-falcon-7x-loss-of-control-after-pitch-trim-runaway
19. BEA report on the Dassault incident (in French): https://www.bea.aero/uploads/tx_elydbrapports/hb-n110525.pdf

"Faulty soldering in an electronic card can lead to wrong information being sent to the flight computer, which then decides to pitch up or bank without it being necessary," Ranter said about the Dassault flight. "In this case, things ended well, but barely."

"Tiny things can have huge consequences," the Aviation Safety Network founder concluded.

Am 6 Februar 1996
stürzte auf dem Flug
nach Deutschland
vor der Küste der
Dominikanischen Republik
ein Flugzeug ins Meer.
Bei diesem Unglück gab
es keine Überlebenden,
und nur 73 Opfer
konnten geborgen werden.
Für 116 Menschen wurde
das Meer zur letzten
Ruhestätte.

Monument to the victims of Birgenair Flight 301.

A Boeing "triple seven" of Malaysian Airlines. In 2005 its ADIRU's broke
down and almost caused a tragedy. (photo: Laurent Errera, Wikicommons)

162

Qantas Airbus 330 involved in nearly fatal nosedive in 2008 because of malfunctioning ADIRU (Flight 72). (photo: Chris Finney, Contrabandit Photos)

Different Adiru's lined up in an Airbus 330. (photo: Amine Mefici)

Newspaper report on Flight 72. (photo: Chris Finney, Contrabandit Photos)

Spanish newspaper reports of the Spanair Flight JK5022 crash in Madrid.

Pilar Vera Palmés (in the middle), president of the organizations of victims of JK5022. On the right, survivor Rafael Vidal. (photo: AVJK5022)

Family members of Spanair crash demonstrate in Las Palmas, May 2017. Nine years after the accident, they demand an independent investigation commission. (photo: AVJK5022)

CHAPTER 7

–

HUMAN ERROR OR FLAWED MACHINES?

The subject of this book – the increasing automation in aviation and the risks this implies – is part of the larger debate on the move toward automation as computers evolve, taking over tasks formerly reserved for human operators.

There is an interesting paradox: The more sophisticated certain automated areas become, the more intricate human intervention becomes. Operational tasks are reduced to a minimum but when intervention is necessary, it tends to be insufficient because the "operator" lacks experience in handling the system manually.

That seems to be the media consensus with regard to the Air France 447 accident, the most emblematic "modern" air disaster. Purportedly, the pilots were not up to the task of controlling a sophisticated aircraft. Thus, we can extrapolate that humans are the weakest link in the chain of decisions and the future of aviation necessarily will be one without pilots.

THE HUMAN FACTOR

Not everybody agrees with this. One of these people is Diego Turjanski, an Argentinean psychologist… and a pilot.

How I found Turjanski was a fortunate coincidence. As I was writing this book, a colleague in a co-working space mentioned that his cousin was a psychologist who works with pilots. His specialty is behavioral safety. I pictured in my mind over-stressed pilots reclining on a sofa and complaining about the workload and their lack of sleep.

"No, it's nothing like that," laughed Turjanski, a man in his late 30s, as we chatted by Skype in March 2017.

Turjanski told me he doesn't treat pilots personally, but he applies his psychology training in accident prevention as a member of the Investigative Board for Aviation Accidents (JIAAC). "But I do understand your confusion. Actually, in psychology there are two prevailing tenets: One seeks to change behavior, and the other accepts that people have a specific personality and seeks to help the individual adapt to the circumstances. I prefer the second option, because I think it's hard to change people."

Why does the Argentinean board of investigation and prevention for aviation accidents employ a psychologist?

Eighty percent of aviation accidents are due to so-called, but badly coined, human errors. So the psychological part of the investigation of accidents becomes very important.

Human error is a familiar concept, but it is actually not that old particularly with regard to aviation.

Throughout the history of commercial aviation we can distinguish three periods during which airline disasters were viewed quite differently. Up until the 70s, most air disasters were linked to technical errors, since there was still a lot of

168

development to do. For instance, airplanes crashed because fuselages exploded.

You are referring to the Comet?"
Yes, exactly (The Comet was an ultramodern de Havilland jet launched in the 1950s that suffered structural problems such as metal fatigue and it disintegrated at high altitudes.)

Then from the 70s on, the view on aircraft disasters changed radically. The Tenerife crash (in which 583 people were killed after a Panam and a KLM -Jumbo jet collided in 1977) was the main reason. After that disaster, the focus on accidents started to change. Huge aircraft crashing on the ground without technical failure on the part of the plane? Nowadays, this might not seem so extraordinary, but in the 70s – in the aircraft industry – it was extremely hard to accept. The amount of money that had been invested in engines and in fuselages, and then one man's actions send that all to the garbage bin. The media took increasing interest in aviation catastrophes and they soon brought the concept of human error in relation to industrial accidents into the mainstream. The term has become accepted by science, but it is a term invented by the media, because of course: all errors are human.

The media identified the KLM pilot as the one to blame in the Tenerife crash, downplaying all the other circumstances.
Exactly. As a result, the focus turned to controlling the *human factor*, rather than technical aspects. At the time, Cockpit Resource Management (CRM - see Glossary page 182) started coming into vogue. And from the 1970s on, most technical

challenges were being overcome. For example, jet engines have improved dramatically and have become extremely reliable. Today we have only 4% so-called purely technical errors leading to accidents.

So reducing human error became the new paradigm in airline safety?
Until the 21st century, this was undeniably the installed philosophy in the aircraft industry. In other words, security can be guaranteed by improving the performance of the first-line actors: air traffic controllers, pilots, dispatchers and so on. So a lot of regulations targeting fatigue, training and internal communications were issued. But surprisingly, this had poor results. Certain errors seemed immune to regulations.

For instance?
Well, like errors of automatisms and communication. So a third model of aeronautical safety surged around 2010, thanks to a pivotal book by James Reason who introduced the so-called *Swiss cheese model of accident causation*[20] which helped to redefine the concept of *human error*.

Like when you line up layers of Swiss cheese, as defense layers, it is not unthinkable that at some point the holes will line up.
Yes. In other words, even though you have many layers of defense, a so-called human error (represented by one of the holes in the Swiss cheese) is one factor, a hole in a layer, you cannot control. An accident is always a consequence of a badly designed system, so it (human error) can trigger the accident but

---

20. "Human Error", by James T. Reason. Cambridge University Press, 1990.

it's never truly the cause. Human error is to aeronautical safety what fever is to the human body: It's a symptom of a flawed security sequence.

So human error would be more like a symptom rather than a cause?
Effectively. The theory of James Reason had its impact on industrial safety as well as aeronautical safety. From the 21st century on, there has been greater emphasis on ergonomics and flight deck design to make it easier to handle. There are still a lot of people who think accidents happen to *people* and not to systems. They argue that the *people* should be more careful.

If we look at the AF447 accident – which I have studied a lot – the consensus seems to be that it was the pilots' mistake. They were unable to fly the plane in Alternate Law without the computer. Others have argued that the co-pilot Bonin was *stressed, that he got scared.* But these explanations still focus on the individual. The official explanations and conclusions don't convince me. People in a workplace situation tend to make rational decisions. When somebody in a cockpit pulls the yoke, the nose goes up. But if you continue to do this, this will provoke a stall. Anybody with 5 hours of flight time knows that. This guy had 3,000 hours! So explanations like "he wasn't aware" or "he got scared" do not suffice, in my opinion.

Also, outsiders often base their judgment on what *the pilot should have done.* That's what we call in psychology a *"hindsight bias"*: When one knows the outcome and says it's obvious this most likely caused the accident. When you don't know the outcome, it's much harder to evaluate a decision.

We cannot fully understand what happened in the cockpit of the AF447. We cannot get in the heads of the pilots. There were things that were already flawed in the design. They were without speed sensors, they were in the dark over the ocean, in the middle of clouds with no Angle of Attack meters. They knew the pitch, but not the Angle of Attack.

So how could the pilots get confused so quickly?
Airbus engineers don't necessarily think of the automatisms of the pilots but of the commercial value, so first and foremost the plane is designed to fly easy. It's a commercial logic. Boeing probably provides more transparency to the operator than Airbus, but it's much easier to fly an Airbus than a Boeing. If you compare the cockpit of an Airbus 320 with that of a Boeing 737, you can see that the latter has buttons and switches everywhere.

There is a lot of criticism about the design of the flying laws – Normal Law, Alternate Law. The pilots of AF447 apparently could not fly in Alternate Law.
The fact that a plane has built-in protections is not bad. What is bad is to think these protections make things completely safe. The protections address certain problems but automatically cause others.

For instance?
Alternate Law introduces a level of complexity in the system, so the system becomes opaque, untransparent to the first-line operator. The pilot asks himself things like "What is the computer doing?"

So are automation and computers systems a threat to passenger safety?
I think automation is really good and can help the human operator in a predictable situation. The Auto Pilot is a great thing. It's impossible to imagine flying a plane manually today, especially for long distances. Imagine being stuck at the yoke for 12 hours… the fatigue, loss of attention.

The problem is when automation tries to "replace" human beings in the decision-making process. Psychologists like Herbert Simon ("Bounded Rationality") or Nobel Prize laureate Daniel Kahneman argue that humans are capable of taking decisions in uncertain and risky situations with considerable success. For poorly defined problems, humans are much better decision makers than computers.

What are some poorly defined problems in aviation?
If you are taking off and an engine catches fire, I would not doubt for a moment that the computer would help there. It is a well-defined problem, so the computer switches the engine off to keep the plane from catching fire. The computer then acts on the controls to correct the asymmetric power of flying with one engine. But a computer works with an algorithm. If A, then B. The computer must be sure A is happening to decide B. And that is not always well-defined.

Take something rather simple such as dodging a storm. A storm is a dynamic event, the storm moves. It's a red spot in front of you and the pilot needs to decide, will I go around here or there. And the decision depends on where one thinks the storm is going. An experienced pilot will say, we will go this way, and if somebody asks why, he says: "I don't know but I think the storm is moving the other way." These things are part of implicit knowledge. And human beings are by definition capable of taking decisions in situations with high levels of uncertainty. And very efficiently. That's why I think we won't have unmanned planes in the future, at least not for a long time.

So are you suggesting computers and a human working together make a good team?
Yes, without a doubt. Because one combines predictability with human talent. On the other hand, the computer is making the pilot lazier. How can the industry address this? By increasing the amount of manual flights for pilots?

The increasing automation in aviation is not a philosophical stance, but the logic of an industry. You can have "Maverick" from Top Gun as a pilot but at what cost? Safety is not as important as the industrial logic, which starts with the customer.

You mean the passenger is part of the problem?
Sure. We have an industry that does not tolerate accidents, but does not tolerate high fares either.

There is a constant trade-off between safety and cost. If you lean too much to one side, you tempt bankruptcy. You lean the other way and you tempt a disaster. Everybody wants to fly safely, but nobody wants to pay more than 30 euros for a ticket from Madrid to Paris.

So every once in a while an air disaster is bound to occur. Did we learn our lesson from the Air France 447 accident?
Actually, two years after the Air France 447 crash, another Air France Airbus (an A340, the four-engine version of the A330)

174

almost flew into a stall. If you read about the incident, it's really incredible. It could have been AF447, almost a carbon copy, two years later. In a patch of turbulence, the crew accidentally disconnected the Auto Pilot. (Turjanski refers to Air France Flight 385 which left from Caracas for Paris at 23:38 UTC, almost identical to AF447, which was flying from Rio to Paris.)

The pilots were not aware that the Auto Pilot was disconnected since the alarm was masked by another alarm, a repetitive chime of overspeed. They kept on flying manually, thinking they were in Auto Pilot. The plane started to climb, reaching a *vertical speed* of 5,700 feet per minute without the crew noticing. At some point the plane lost speed.

A QUESTION OF FATE

According to the BEA report on Flight AF385, the aircraft reached an altitude of 38,150 feet. The speed had fallen to 226 knots, or 20 knots below minimum speed. The Pilot Flying then ordered the Auto Pilot to descend (using the altitude selection knob), but when the plane did not react and there was no information on the Primary Flight Display, he realized the Auto Pilot was disconnected and he lowered the pitch manually.

The BEA incident report[21] specifies that there was a problem with the alarms. The alarm warning about the Auto Pilot disconnection should not have been masked by a master caution related to overspeed. According to the French Safety Bureau "the Airbus model 340 was certified in 1995, but the

---

21. For the full report: https://www.bea.aero/fileadmin/documents/docspa/2011/f-zu110722.en/pdf/f-zu110722.en.pdf

superposition of alarm signals is not up-to-date with current certification standards." The BEA comment is a nod to the AF447 accident, when the stall alarm did not work properly. "Luckily the crew noticed and lowered the pitch attitude (Angle of Attack) of the plane," Turjanski said. "Just a little longer and the machine would have entered into a stall."

Turjanski acknowledges that "the BEA wrote an interesting report, because it did not blame the pilots – the easy way out – while it did perform a true systemic analysis." Even so, the BEA did not seem to consider this incident to be overly dramatic. "All's well that ends well," the BEA seems to think.

The last line in the 2011 Air France incident report reads: "The flight continued without further incident to Paris-Charles de Gaulle airport, where the crew landed at 8:33."

Exactly what should have happened with Air France Flight 447.

BASIC AVIATION TERMINOLOGY
USED IN THIS BOOK

A

ADIRU: Air data inertial reference unit (ADIRU) supplies air data (airspeed, angle of attack and altitude) and inertial reference (position and attitude) information to the pilots' electronic flight instrument system displays as well as other systems on the aircraft such as the engines, autopilot, aircraft flight control system and landing gear systems. It may be backed up by secondary unit (SAARU).

Aircraft Communication Addressing and Reporting System (ACARS): a digital datalink system for transmission of short messages between aircraft and ground stations, using a radio or a satellite connection. Before ACARS, all communication between the aircraft and ground personnel was performed through VHF radios. ACARS messages can be directed either to Air Traffic Control or to the base of the airline, for maintenance purposes for instance. Although there have been arguments to convert the ACARS into an on-line black box, this has not been implemented. For now, the ACARS-messages contain a limited amount of the flight's parameters.

Air Traffic Control (ATC): a ground-based control primary purpose is to prevent collisions, organize air traffic, and provide information for pilots.

Airspeed Indicator (ASI): an instrument used in an aircraft to display the airspeed (in knots). On a large aircraft, the ASI is part of the PFD, located on the left side of the artificial horizon display. Generally there is another analogue ASI ona a stand-by instrument.

Airworthiness Directive (AD): a notification to owners and operators of certified aircraft that a known safety deficiency with a particular model of aircraft, engine, avionics or other system exists and must be corrected. A failure to correct an outstanding AD affects the airworthiness of the aircraft. AD's are issued by the National Civil Aviation Authorities like the FAA (US) or the EASA (Europe).

Altimeter: There are two types of altimeters on an airplane.
The barometric altimeter works with air pressure and measures the difference between the current atmospheric pressure and the pressure at sea level.
The radar altimeter on the other hand, measures altitude by using beams or radio waves which reflect off the ground. The radar altimeter is the basis for the Ground Warning Proximity System (GWPS).

Angle of Attack (AOA) is the angle between the wing and the oncoming air or relative wind. The angle of attack can be

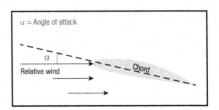

simply described as the difference between where a wing is pointing and where it is going. An increase in angle of attack results in an increase of lift. Too high an angle of attack can lead to a Stall (see definition of Stall)

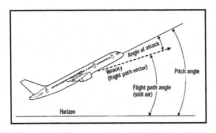

The Angle of Attack should not be confused with **Pitch Attitude**, which is the relationship between the longitudinal axis of the plane and a chosen reference, like the horizon. Although an increase of pitch will often result in an increased angle of attack (as was the case on the AF447), these are two different concepts. The Angle of Attack depends on the *relative* wind (which as the word relative implies, is unpredictable), elementary to create lift. The AOA is measured by the Angle of Attack sensors.

Angle of Attack Sensors: Vane like devices attached to the fuselage to measure the angle of attack.

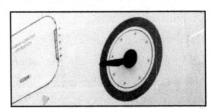

Angle of Attack sensor on Airbus 330

Atmospheric Pressure at Sea Level (QNH): This is used to adjust the scale of the barometric altimeter for elevation, taking the sea level as a reference.

Attitude: see Pitch attitude

Autopilot (A/P): The autopilot assists the operator in controlling the aircraft, allowing him/her to focus on other aspects of operation, like the weather or communication with Air Traffic Control.

Auto Thrust or Autothrottle (A/THR): A power setting of an aircraft's engines by specifying a desired flight characteristic, rather than manually controlling the fuel flow. This conserves fuel and extends engine life by calculating the right amount of fuel required to attain a target indicated air speed.

Avionics: This term is a blend of *aviation* and *electronics* and refers to all the electronic devices and computers installed on a modern aircraft.

Auxiliary Power Unit (APU): The primary purpose of an aircraft APU is to provide power to start the main engines. APUs are also used to run accessories while the engines are shut down. This allows the cabin to be comfortable while the passengers are boarding and to run systems for preflight checks.

C

Cockpit Voice Recorder (CVR): Records the conversations of pilots in the cockpit.

Flight Data Recorder (FDR): Records specific aircraft performance parameters. The recordings of CVR and FDR are found on the so-called black box, orange in color.

Centralized Fault Display System (CFDS): Diagnostic device of an Airbus, which identifies a faulty system and reports this to the pilots through the ECAM or to the maintenance crew.

Cockpit Resources Management (CRM) aims to optimize the communication between crew members so to enhance situational awareness and avoid accidents.

Cumulonimbus cloud (CB): also known as *Charlie Bravo* in aviation slang is a towering vertical cloud associated with thunderstorms. They can be very dangerous to air traffic, not so much because of the turbulence but because of he secondary effects like hail or sudden changes in temperatures, which can affect external sensors.

Circuit Breaker (CB): a switch designed to protect an electrical circuit from damage caused by excess current, typically resulting from an overload or short circuit. Its function is to interrupt current flow after a fault and can be reset.

E

Electronic Centralized Aircraft Monitoring (ECAM): This system provides display and monitoring of aircraft systems on an Airbus. It is displayed in the centre of the instrument panel and includes alerts and checklists. The information on the ECAM comes from two **Flight Warning Computers** (FWC's). On Boeing and Embraer planes, this very same system is called EICAS (Engine Indicating and Crew Alerting System).

F

Flight Crew Operating Manual (FCOM): is a publication with system descriptions, emergency procedures and performance data. It is the primary flight crew reference for the operation of an aircraft.

Flight Management Computer (FMC): A computer system that replaced the flight engineer and executes a wide variety of in-flight tasks, like the management of the Flight Plan (the trayectory of the aircraft), reducing considerably the workload of the flight crew.

Flight Control Computer: On a modern aircraft, there are more than 300 computers. As we cannot mention them all in this book, we will highlight a few important ones, taking as an example the Airbus 320, the plane involved in the Air Asia Q8501 crash.

On an Airbus 320 the flight controls are controlled by 7 computers: 2 Elevator Aileron Computers (**ELAC**), 2 Flight Augmentation Computers (**FAC**) and 3 Spoiler Elevator Computers (**SEC**). These computers process the inputs of the pilot's sidestick or the Flight Management and Guidance System or FMGS (when on Autopilot, which is most of the time) and pass on the right orders to the aircraft's control surfaces, such as rudder, elevator, ailerons. These 7 computers are redundant, meaning that if ELAC 1 would fail, ELAC 2 takes over.

The first computer is known as the Primary Flight Control Computer (PRIM) and the back-up computer as the Secondary Flight Control Computer (SEC).

Flight Director (FD): A display consisting of a horizontal and a vertical command bar on the primary flight display (PFD). The command bars are generated by the flight management computer and provide pitch and roll guidance to the pilot to follow, identical to the commands the autopilot follows when it is on. The Flight Director and Auto Pilot are usually both on in flight.

Flight Level (FL): Altitude level at standard pressure, expressed in hundreds of feet. E.g FL100 is 10.000 feet.

Fly-By-Wire (FBW): means that the mechanical linkage between control column and control surface has been replaced by electrical wires.

G

Ground Proximity Warning System (GPWS): is an alert system to warn pilots if their aircraft is in imminent danger of hitting the ground or an obstacle. It depends on the radar altimeter, basically a sensor which sends out radio waves and measures the time it takes for these waves to return.

I

Indicated Air Speed (IAS): The airspeed measured by the dynamic pressure of the outside air entering a pitot tube. The different control speeds of an airplane are measured in knots.

Inter-Tropical Convergence Zone (ITCZ): A band of thunderstorms around the equator, caused by the convergence of the northeast and southeast trade winds. Among sailors the ITCZ was known as "the doldrums". The ITCZ is important for aviation since the cloud cover is higher and the storms are difficult to avoid.

L

Lift, Weight, Thrust and Drag: the four aerodynamic forces acting upon an aircraft. Lift is the opposite force of Weight and Thrust the opposite force of Drag.

Loss of Control in Flight (LOC-I): Accidents or incidents in which the flight crew is unable to maintain control of the aircraft in flight. In the 21st century, LOC-I has become the most important cause of air disasters, partly because other types of accidents have been reduced (due to more reliable communications and better materials) and because of the increased dependence on computers that govern modern Fly-by-Wire aircraft.

M

Minimum Equipment List (MEL): Minimum requirements for a flight to be released, in spite of inoperative equipment, to avoid revenue loss to the operator and discomfort to the passengers.

N

Nautical Mile (NM): A nautical mile is a unit of measurement, corresponds to 1852 meters or 6,000 feet.

P

Pilot in Command (PIC) or Captain.
Second in Command (SIC) or First Officer. He is also referred to as the Co-Pilot. The SIC is perfectly capacitated to fly the plane, as well as the Captain. Modern aircrafts are equipped for two pilots with identical instruments panels so they can switch between the two.

Pilot Flying (PF): Pilot who is actually flying the plane. Could be either the PIC or the SIC.

Pilot Not Flying (PNF) or Pilot Monitoring: The pilot who is performing other tasks.

Pitch, Roll and Yaw: Since an aircraft move in three-dimensional space (unlike a car on the road, which moves in two-dimensional space) there are three basic movements for an aircraft to change its position towards the incoming airflow.

Roll is the rotation around the longitudinal axis: wings tilt up or down
Yaw is the rotation around the vertical axis: nose left or nose right.

Pitch up/down is the rotation around the transversal axis: nose up or nose down.

The pitch or **pitch attitude** of an aircraft relative to the horizon is observed on the attitude indicator (which also displays the roll angle). This attitude indicator is known as the *artificial horizon* and works with a gyroscope flywheel.

Analogue artificial horizon   Digital artificial horizon on PFD

Pitot Tube (or pressure head) is a 18th century invention of a French scientist (Henri Pitot) to measure fluid flow velocity. It can be used to determine the speed of an aircraft as the speed of a boat in the water. On an aircraft the pitot tubes are attached

along the axis of the aircraft, facing forward. The pressure measured in the tube is a combination of static pressure and pressure due to the aircraft forward speed.

Pitot tube on a Boeing 737, above: the AOA indicator

Primary Flight Display (PFD): An integrated display which includes attitude, airspeed, heading, altitude, vertical speed and auto flight information.

Protections: Limitations set for a Fly-by-Wire aircraft (when flying in Normal Law) to prevent it from exceeding its aerodynamic limits. These protections are also known as the "flight envelope".

Q

QRH: The Quick Reference Handbook contains all the procedures applicable for abnormal and emergency conditions in an easy-to-use format. The QRH also contains performance data of the aircraft and the checklists. In case the plane is fitted with an ECAM (or EICAS) the QRH is used a back-up.

R

RTLU: Rudder Travel Limiter Unit: Its function is not to move the rudder but to limit excessive inputs on the rudder and the vertical stabilizer and thus excessive yaw movements within the flight envelope.

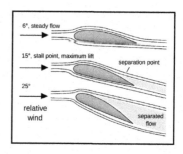

S

Stall: An airplane flies because of an elementary aerodynamic principle, explained in the laws of Bernouilli: The incoming airflow on an airfoil creates lift, as the fillets of air on top of the airfoil (in a raindrop shape) will pass faster than the ones underneath the airfoil, thus creating reduced air pressure on top of the wing.

Now when the Angle of Attack is too high, the fillets of air will be separated from the wing and not be able to create lift.

Signals of a stalling plane is heavy buffeting before the plane starts to fall.

T

Traffic alert and Collision Avoidance System (TCAS) is an aircraft collision avoidance system designed to reduce the incidence of mid-air collisions between aircraft. It monitors the airspace around an aircraft for other aircraft equipped with a corresponding active transponder.

Take Off/Go Around (TOGA): The full forward thrust lever position.

Flex and Max continuous (FLX and MCT): Reduced power setting but still more thrust than in Climb. FLX and MCT are applied when flying with one engine.

Climb (CL): climb position is the power setting the aircraft will use most of the flight.

0 position: When thrust levers are in idle.

U

Unreliable Air Speed (UAS): A situation where erroneous air speed indications are displayed on the instruments, which are likely to confuse the pilots. These UAS may be caused by malfunctioning external sensors like clogged pitots or static ports. A failure to promptly recognize and respond to erroneous flight instrument indications, could result in loss of control in flight (LOC-I).

On a Fly-By-Wire aircraft, UAS may cause be the degradation of the Flight Laws with less envelope protections. The Autopilot and Autothrust may also be disconnected after UAS. Pilots are trained in simulators to apply the right procedure for unreliable speed situations.

Coordinated Universal Time (UTC): UTC is a time standard derived from the Greenwich meridian time zone. Basically UTC coincides with the time in London, while for instance New York is located in the UTC-4 timezone (four hours behind of London) and Melbourne in the UTC+10 zone, 10 hours ahead of London.

V

Vertical Speed (VS): The rate of climb or descent of an aircraft. It is measured by a Vertical Speed Indicator. On a modern Flight Display, the vertical speed is on the right side, next to the Altimeter.

ORGANIZATIONS
AND INSTITUTIONS

EASA: European Aviation Safety Agency: European authority that regulates all aspects of civil aviation.

FAA: Federal Aviation Administration: US authority that regulates all aspects of civil aviation.

ICAO: International Civil Aviation Organization is a UN-organization with headquarters in Montreal, Canada. In 1999, within the ICAO member states, the Montreal convention was adopted by which financial compensation for victims of air disasters was established.

Montreal Convention (1999): This ICAO convention replaces the Warsaw Convention and sets provisions for victims of air disasters. The convention sets a minimum compensations of 100,000 Special Drawing Rights of the IMF ($50,000 US dollars, $200,000 US dollars, etc). This means the airline is strictly liable for these amounts. For higher amounts, the airline can pass liability on to third parties. The compensations for victims' family members is subject to their economic dependency of the victim. After the AF447 crash, for instance, some family members that depended directly on the victims received around $200,000 US dollars, while other close family members, received less than $50,000 US dollars.

NATIONAL SAFETY BOARDS

AAIB: The British Air Accident Investigation Branch of the UK.

ATSB: Australian Transport Safety Bureau.

BFU: Bundesstelle für Flugunfalluntersuchung (German Investigation Agency of Aviation Accidents).

BEA: Bureau d'Enquêtes et d'Analyses (French Investigation Agency of Aviation Accidents).

CIAIAC: Comisión de Investigación de Accidentes e Incidentes de Aviación Civil (Spanish Civil Aviation Accident Investigation Commission).

DGAC: Dirección General de Aeronáutica Civil (Aeronautical Board of the Dominican Republic).

JIAAC: Junta de Investigación de Accidentes de Aviación Civil (Civil Aviation Accident Investigation Board of Argentina).

KNKT: Komite National Keselamatan Transpotasi (Indonesian Investigation Agency of Aviation Accidents).

NTSB: National Transportation Safety Board (US).

I would like to thank those people whose support was fundamental for the publication of this book.

Editor: Tom Buckley
Production manager: Teresa León
Proofreaders: Malcolm Gibson-Yooll, Patricia Mathews
and Menno Stuart.

The Patrons: Tom Casaer, Koen Christiaen,
Ellen Dieusaert, Antoon Dieusaert, Karl Dieusaert,
Erik Lesire, Teresina Papaleo, Hilda Van Pelt.

Video: Gabriel Miguel, Felipe Rugeles,
Mercedes Pérez-Van Rey.

The pilots of Aerolineas Argentinas:
Alejandro López Camelo (ALPA), Luis Iglesias (Cefebra),
Alejandro Covello, Tomás Wechsler, Carlos Hansen.

Victims Families Organizations: Maarten Van Sluys,
Laurent Lamy, Dirk Peter, Pilar Vera Palmés.

Lightning Source UK Ltd.
Milton Keynes UK
UKOW04f0814171117
312878UK00001B/288/P